LANZAROTE & WINE
LANDSCAPE AND CULTURE

Rubén Acosta - Mario Ferrer

⊙ ediciones **remotas**

Production:
Ediciones Remotas

Printing:
Lugami Artes Gráficas

© Copyright Photographs:
Rubén Acosta
Except: Teodoro Maisch (p. 22), Martín Arteta (p. 24), Rafael Silva (p. 27), Nicolás Melián
(p. 33), Leandro Viera (p. 55), Christian Piesch (p. 89), Janire Villaverde (p. 89), Carlos
Martínez (p. 86), Ignacio Romero (p. 103), Joaquín García Vera (p. 106), Adriel Perdomo
(p. 106) and Miguel Cabrera (p. 109). Images provided by kind permission of Antonio Lorenzo
(p. 30, 31, 67), Bodegas El Grifo (p. 84-95), Bodegas Rubicón (p. 90-91), Bodegas La Geria
(p. 87, 108), Museo Tanit (p. 98) and Museo el Patio (p. 98).

© Illustrations:
Santiago Alemán p. 46, 48-49, 51-53, 62.
César Mánrique Foundation p. 66.

© Text:
Rubén Acosta and Mario Ferrer
Except: Juan José Otamendi (p. 13-29), Agustín Pallarés (p. 35-36), Ignacio Romero (p. 43-44,
100-102), Alberto González (p. 57-61), Ignacio Valderas (p. 71), Gustavo Palomo (p. 78-79).

© Design:
Rubén Acosta
Layout: Natividad Betancor

Translation: Samantha Coker

Copyright of current edition:
Ediciones Remotas
C/ Tirso de Molina nº 6, 1p
35500 Arrecife - Lanzarote
www.edicionesremotas.com

ISBN: 978-84-945717-1-8

Legal deposit: GC 853-2016

First edition: October 2016

Printed in Spain

This book is dedicated to the farm workers of Lanzarote. To the men and women who managed to triumph over adversity and overcome the ravages of volcanic eruptions and drought to produce a truly unique cultural landscape which must be protected.

THE AUTHORS

Rubén Acosta

Rubén holds a Bachelor of Arts degree in Audiovisual Communication and a Masters in Photography and Cultural Engineering. He is a freelance photographer and cultural consultant involved in the revitalisation of La Geria with projects such as the 'We are La Geria - Cultural Action Plan'. He is an award-winning international artist and has exhibited his work in events such as *Photoespaña*. He comes from a family of long wine making traditions with vineyards in La Geria that produce artisan wines.

Mario Ferrer

Mario holds a Doctorate and Bachelor's degree in Journalism and History of Art. He is a prolific writer and has published many research papers in magazines and scientific conferences, as well as numerous popular interest titles. His specialist fields include contemporary history, journalism and culture and he has worked as editor, exhibition curator and digital archive expert (he coordinates Lanzarote's Memoriadelanzarote.com). Mario also authored the report on La Geria that was Lanzarote's entry in the European Landscape Award in 2013.

CONTRIBUTORS

Santiago Alemán

Illustrator and painter born in Lanzarote, author of various books including *Tesoros de la isla* or 'Island Treasures'. Professor of drawing at the Pancho Lasso School of Art in Arrecife.

Juan José Otamendi

Co-owner of Bodegas El Grifo winery together with his brother Fermín. He manages the library in the Wine Museum and has published numerous works on the island's viticulture.

Gustavo Palomo

Sommelier trained at the Madrid Chamber of Commerce, holds a Masters in Oenology, finalist in the Golden Nose Sommelier Competition (Nariz de Oro) in 2011, finalist at the Madrid Fusión Congress and two-time winner of the best sommelier in the Canaries award in 2010 and in 2012.

Alberto González

Born in La Gomera, he is an agricultural engineer and oenologist and holds a Masters in Viticulture and Oenology. In 2012 he came second in the Best Oenologists in Spain awards and was positioned in the top ten best oenologists in the world, holding sixth place in 2012.

Ignacio Romero

Holds a degree in Environmental Biology from the University of La Laguna and a Masters in Environmental Resource Management from Granada University. He is at the forefront of a movement to raise awareness about Lanzarote's social and environmental concerns by means of his organisation called *Senderismo Lanzarote*.

Ignacio Valderas

Director and oenologist for the Bodegas Los Bermejos winery with more than 20 years experience in Lanzarote's wine making sector.

Agustín Pallarés

Researcher and investigator in the fields of Lanzarote prehistory, history and toponymy. Further information about his work and publications can be found on agustinpallares.blogspot.com.es

INDEX

1. LANZAROTE - A UNIQUE TERRITORY

Lanzarote is an island that evokes a mythical age; an extraordinary place on earth where the natural elements of water, earth, air and fire converge. It is the setting for Timanfaya's open air museum of volcanoes that exhibits its undeniable might over the landscape. It is a place where rock becomes sculpture and the terrain is transformed into a work of art.

The origin of the Fire Mountains dates back to that fateful day in 1730 when Lanzarote's history would change forever. The island faced one of the most powerful series of volcanic eruptions to be experienced in this part of the world in many centuries. The parish priest of Yaiza, Lorenzo Curbelo, left what has become legendary testimony as to what took place: "*On 1st September 1730, between nine and ten at night, the ground opened up in Timanfaya, two leagues from Yaiza... and an enormous mountain rose up from the bowels of the earth.*"

For a period of six years, until 1736, the volcanoes became a part of daily life on the island and eventually covered nearly a third of its surface area. Lanzarote had been shaken to the core with what seemed at first dire consequences for the island's modest economy, but out of the destruction came a resurrection of fortunes thanks to the natural properties of the volcanic ash, or *lapilli* (locally known as *picón*, *rofe* or *sand*). Farming using this *rofe* was known to have been used prior to the eruptions

but it was at this point that its use became widespread and would stamp its mark on the island's wine growing industry. Besides Timanfaya, the island boasts many unique areas, including Europe's second largest Marine Reserve comprised of five small islets located in the north of the island. This part of the island is also home to the Cliffs of Famara and the Volcán de la Corona volcano, two spectacular mountain regions that date from different eras with picturesque villages and stunning beaches nestled at their feet. As you explore the historical town of the Villa of Teguise towards the centre of the island you can clearly see the surrounding areas of El Jable. *Jable* is the local name given to the coarse white sand found in this area and which extends in a wide corridor from the north to the south of the island.

The centre of the island is home to two main attractions in the shape of La Geria and Timanfaya where you can also see spectacular landmarks like El Golfo, Las Salinas de Janubio and the Hervideros or 'Boiling Pots'. Along the island's leeward coast lie the main tourist resorts and residential areas. The majority of the population is concentrated in the coastal stretch from Costa Teguise to Puerto Calero, whilst much smaller farming hamlets or fishing villages can be found dotted throughout the rest of the island.

The Atlantic Ocean brings its influence to bear in the south of Lanzarote where

9

A Biosphere Reserve for more than two decades

On 7th October 1993 UNESCO declared Lanzarote a Biosphere Reserve. This prestigious international award recognised the efforts made by Lanzarote society to find a harmonious balance between economic progress and respect for the island's natural surroundings. The unique region of La Geria played an important role in Lanzarote being made a Biosphere Reserve, together with the network of Centres of Art, Culture and Tourism as well as the island's pioneering urban planning schemes.

The concept of a Biosphere Reserve was devised by UNESCO in 1976 to recognise and protect highly emblematic ecosystems. The inclusion of Lanzarote in the network of Biosphere Reserves was a hugely important step as it was the first time that a territory had been chosen as a whole unit (including the residential areas, infrastructures, equipment etc.) with the idea that Lanzarote would become an experimental laboratory of sustainability. Like all laboratories, it has witnessed failures as well as successes which have given way to much social and political debate, but which have also served to raise greater awareness.

visitors can take a boat trip and explore the Isla de Lobos islet or venture a little further afield to nearby Fuerteventura, an island famed for its incredible beaches. The south of Lanzarote is also home to the idyllic white sandy bays of Papagayo which lie beneath the Natural Monument of Los Ajaches; a relatively low-lying mountain range which makes for perfect hiking territory. Some 42.1% of the island's land comes under the protection of some kind of territorial or environmental law.

An International Economy

Since the Spanish conquest at the beginning of the fifteenth century, (it was the first island to be conquered in 1402) the Canarian economy has hinged on international factors, especially in Europe, the main market for agricultural exports, but also in America and Africa. Whilst wine enjoyed an essential role in the island's economy in the 18th century, in the centuries that followed the export market was to swing from buoyancy to periods of crisis brought about by a virtual total decline in some of the island's produce. Lanzarote and Fuerteventura had once been known as the 'barn of the Canaries' due to their prolific production of cereals, but they eventually suffered the trials and tribulations of an age-old fragile economy. They were islands caught up in the negative cycle of being subject to their geographic isolation in the Atlantic ocean as well as being at the mercy of its arid land and the lack of adequate infrastructure. It was only thanks to the export of produce such as natural dyes produced such things as dyes produced from orchella weed and cochineal that the population managed to avoid total emigration. The scarce wealth that did exist on the island was in the hands of a small elite of landowners.

The second half of the twentieth century saw the modernisation of fishing methods

MAP OF PROTECTED NATURAL AREAS

0 Parque nacional de Timanfaya

1 Reserva Marina de Los Islotes

2 Parque Natural del Archipiélago Chinijo

3 Parque Natural de Los Volcanes

4 Monumento Natural del Malpais de la Corona

5 Monumento natural de Los Ajaches

6 Paisaje Protegido de La Geria

7 Monumento Natural del Islote de Los Halcones

8 Monumento Natural de Montañas del Fuego

9 Paisaje Protegido de Tenegüime

10 Monumento Nat. de La Cueva de Los Naturalistas

11 Sitio de Interés Científico de Jameos del Agua

12 Sitio de Interés Científico de Las Salinas del Janubio

LANZAROTE DATA (2015)

Resident population:	143,738
Overseas Resident population:	32,003
Nº of tourists:	2,640,862
Nº passengers moving through the airport:	5,334,598
Surface area (km²):	845.9
Protected Areas (km²):	42.1%

Photograph of Jameos del Agua, one of César Manrique's creations, depicting the lake which is home to the island's endemic species of blind albino crab.

and this sector experienced a period of real growth with Arrecife becoming one of the world's most important sardine ports. At the same time, Europe's first desalination plant, capable of providing a public water supply, was installed on the island. This was a momentous technological milestone for the island as it meant that it no longer had to live under the constant threat of water shortages which had left such a mark on the socio-economic development of the island up until that point. During this same period, the island's council, *Cabildo*, together with the artist César Manrique and a wonderful team of collaborators, began work on creating the network of innovative Centres of Art, Culture and Tourism (CACT) in stunning natural locations. This network created the island's model for tourism based on respect for the surrounding environment. The CACT are Lanzarote's standard bearer, representing a world-class tourist destination which receives nearly two million visitors every year.

A fusion of cultures

Geographically speaking, the Canary Islands are strategically positioned at a point where cultural influences from Europe, the Americas and Africa intersect. The climate brings with it an almost daily reminder of its proximity to the African continent which is where the ancient inhabitants, called *Majos*, originally came from, as did many of the pirates who were responsible for attacking the island over the centuries. The island has also enjoyed important socio-economic ties with Africa in the past, especially with the fishing sector, and nowadays it is considered an ideal place for Canarian companies to grow internationally.

Columbus passed through the Canaries on his way to America and in so doing inaugurated a sailing passage that has been crucial to the islands' development. For centuries, Cuba, Venezuela or Uruguay were the main places to which many islanders would emigrate; to such an extent, in fact, that many family ties and economic and social links with South America still endure today. It is the cultural ties that are especially important to the island, as it has been heavily influenced by the language and musical traditions of South America.

It was Europe that brought the islands their conquerors in the 15th century, but it was also Europe that has been responsible for bringing the most significant economic and political influences in the islands' histories. All the new ideas and technology that Europe has exported to the rest of the world, it also shared with the Canary Islands - geographically distant they may be, but the relationship is one of close neighbours. Apart from the Spanish mainland, the Canarian archipelago has experienced historical periods of close ties with other European countries such as France, Portugal and especially the United Kingdom. Currently in Lanzarote alone nearly 15% of the population (20,233 people) is comprised of citizens from other countries in the European Union. Canarian society and culture are the product of a wealth of foreign influences but the islands and their people have evolved their own typically idiosyncratic nature.

One of the greatest challenges Lanzarote society faces today is to attain sustainable development in all aspects of island life. Sustainability has long been a natural approach farmers have used in their connection to and respect for the land and surroundings, which is something César Manrique recognised and understood very clearly. Recent decades have seen clear economic progress but it has been such a fast process that its cultural and social repercussions have not been entirely positive. Employment, energy, economic diversification, the environment and multicultural coexistence are just a few of the inevitable challenges that the island faces in the future.

The Largest Marine Reserve in Europe

The Islotes Marine Reserve is located in the north of the island and comprises some of Lanzarote as well as the five smaller islets of La Graciosa, Alegranza, Montaña Clara, Roque del Este and Roque del Oeste. It's the largest marine reserve in Europe and many specialists agree that it fulfils all the necessary requirements to be declared a National Park. La Graciosa is the only inhabited island and can be reached via ferry from the small harbour town of Órzola. It has just one main village and is the ideal place to enjoy nature, open air sports and a peace and quiet that is hard to find in other places. This marine reserve is noted for its natural features and landscape. The impressive cliff of Famara, which is several kilometres in length, is home to more endemic species (plant, bird and wildlife) per square kilometre than any other place in Europe. The islets are inhabited by such a rich variety of unique birdlife that renowned international scientists carry out research there and the entire area is also greatly valued by marine life experts, particularly specialists in cetaceans.

13

2. WINE IN LANZAROTE

Exceptional Wine

There are many reasons why wine produced on Lanzarote is exceptional:

Firstly is the fact that the Canaries is the most southerly wine growing region before reaching South Africa. Secondly, Lanzarote produces the first grape harvest of the year in Europe. Furthermore, the region has to contend with harsh weather conditions that bring an average rainfall of just 100 litres per square metre, making it less favourable than any other growing region in the world - all these factors lead to the conclusion that, indeed, wine produced on Lanzarote is exceptional.

Given such problematic conditions, it only follows that the techniques used to grow grapes in Lanzarote are also unique and extraordinary. The vine is planted in the fertile soil beneath the layer of volcanic ash and has to be protected from the trade winds with the help of a low semi-circular wall made from volcanic rocks. The gaps between these rocks allow the tempered winds to provide just enough vital ventilation to prevent fungal growth and disease.

This unique method of grape growing which local farmers have had to devise to make the most of the agricultural potential of the island, entails constant laborious and delicate maintenance. So delicate is their care, in fact, that many refer to the island's farmers as 'gardeners' and 'caretakers of the countryside'.

The low production per hectare which is generally between 1,000 kg and 1,500 kg is due to low density planting. The vines are cared for almost exclusively by hand and are constantly subject to the threat of the great nemesis of farmers on Lanzarote; heat waves.

In the La Geria region all the vine tending is carried out manually following the traditional methods handed down for almost three centuries. The farmer of old would have had to create the system of pits and protective walls exclusively by hand or with the help of the camel, his main farming tool. In this way the Lanzarote farmer has transformed thousands of hectares of land since the 18th century. La Geria which is a Natural Protected Landscape is in many ways a very humanised landscape in the sense that it has been extensively shaped by man. However this handling is so respectful towards its surroundings that it is an example of conservation and environmental regeneration. Unaware of the conceptual implications, perhaps, the Lanzarote farmer unwittingly created a paradigm of sustainable farming.

The unique characteristics of grape growing in Lanzarote set it apart from other regions. Lanzarote wines are rather miraculous in that they are born of having to adapt to

15

volcanic tragedy and extreme conditions. This is what lends them their unique qualities and subtleties of flavour and what has given rise to an idiosyncratic landscape with an inherently unique social dimension.

Lapilli - a natural moisture reserve

The series of volcanic eruptions that took place on the island between 1730 and 1736 generated an enormous number of pyroclastic rocks, or volcanic ash, which covered some of the island's most fertile valleys, especially to the south of the eruptions where the north-easterly trade winds blow. This volcanic gravel-like ash, or *lapilli*, is known locally in the Canaries as *picón*, and on Lanzarote it is more commonly referred to as *rofe* or *arena*. It is the essential element needed to cover the fertile soil. This technique which became ever more popular after the eruptions and was used in all types of farming had a range of unique benefits; some derived from its mulching effect (or protective insulation for the fertile soil) and others from the properties of the volcanic material itself. The *rofe* acts as a natural reserve that collects the moisture from the dew, prevents soil erosion, is rich in minerals, prevents moisture from evaporating and also keeps the vines free from disease. In addition, the black colour of the *rofe* absorbs more of the sun's heat which raises the soil temperature compared to the atmospheric temperature. This warmer temperature encourages growth and increases the levels of sugars in the grapes and therefore the level of alcohol.

Using *rofe* as a form of mulch on top of the fertile soil requires a series of extra maintenance work which the vinedresser has to carry out from time to time. This typically entails fertilising or re-defining the pits when the *rofe* starts to collapse, ensuring the plant does not get buried.

Work on the surrounding farmlands can cause the pits, or hollows to cave in. When this occurs, the *rofe* has to be re-dug by hand.

Ungrafted rootstock

One of the other features common to all the wine growing regions on the island is the varieties of grapevines that can be planted. As in the rest of the Canaries, the vines are ungrafted which means that both the rootstock and the vine itself belong to the same grape variety. This is only possible thanks to the fact that the Canaries remained unaffected by the phylloxera blight that ravaged vineyards in Europe. Being islands, Lanzarote and the rest of the Canaries escaped this plague of root louse that devastated grape harvests throughout Europe at the end of the 19th century and beginning of the 20th century. This means the vines are whole and are planted on their own roots without needing to resort to inserting grafts on American vines which

Section cut of a vine which shows the different components that make up grape cultivation in Lanzarote, the layer of *rofe* on top of the fertile soil and the ungrafted vine.

proved to be the only variety resistant to phylloxera. This means that Lanzarote vines are purer and live longer which, in turn, increases their viability and quality when it comes to producing an excellent wine at the end of the process.

The Malvasía Volcánica Grape

The Malvasia grape originates from Asia Minor and Greece and is probably more than 2,000 years old. It was introduced to the Canaries in the 16th century, firstly in Tenerife and then later in other places like La Palma among other varieties brought in from the Mediterranean. It was not to reach Lanzarote's shores until the beginning of the 19th century, however, as up until that time it was the Palomino (*Listán Blanca)* that dominated grape harvests on the island. But the Malvasia's evolution as a result of the island's unique conditions prompted the International Organisation of Vine and Wine (O.I.V.) to officially recognise Malvasía Volcánica as a variety in its own right. This Malvasía Volcánica together with the Malvasía of La Palma (also known as Malvasía Aromática or Auténtica) are the two main varieties of Malvasia in the Canaries.

The Malvasía Volcánica grape is small and low yielding but high quality because of its balance, flavour and perfume which transfer to the wines made with it. Many of

Drying process to make naturally sweet Malvasía wines.

EL GRIFO

CANARI

DESDE 1775

Shakespeare and Malvasía

"*You have a taste for the wine of the Canaries and I too.*" Shakespeare mentioned Malvasia wine which he called 'Canary' or 'Sack', throughout the play *Henry IV*.

This wine made from Malvasia grapes and probably fortified in England, was known for its healing properties in the 17th century and indeed used in the treatment of a range of illnesses and ailments.

The sweet Malvasía wine sometimes called, 'Canary' or 'malmsey' has been referred to in other literary works such as Shakespeare's *Merry Wives of Windsor* and in works by Sir Walter Scott, Robert Louis Stevenson, Lord Byron, Edgar Rice Burroughs, Immanuel Kant and even Giacomo Casanova.

This wine's popularity was at its peak in the 17th century but then it began to decline due to political changes and the rise in popularity of Portugal's wines, especially its Port wine. During this period in history, Canarian wines were produced in Tenerife or in La Palma. It was not until the 18th century that grapes and Malvasia wine reached Lanzarote, after the eruptions of 1730-1736.

By way of a homage to this wine, the El Grifo winery (the oldest remaining winery in the Canaries) is currently producing a sweet white wine called 'Canari' which has been made using the same techniques and blending an assemblage of vintages from 1956, 1970 and 1997.

Re-digging the *rofe* gravel to prevent the vine from being buried.

Lanzarote's vineyards produce white wines using this variety. You can find young dry Malvasia, sweet Malvasia, naturally sweet Malvasia, semi-sweet Malvasia, and dry, oak-fermented Malvasia; their alcohol content varies between 10.5% and 14.5%.

Artisanal and sustainable work

Now, in the early 21st century society across the globe is searching for a means of ensuring sustainable exploitation of the planet's natural resources; hoping to find a means to avoid exhausting our natural surroundings and create a formula that combines long-term socio-economic benefits for mankind, with respect for environmental conservation. Lanzarote has set a clear precedent for the success of this magic formula, especially in its grape growing. The area of La Geria, which has been Lanzarote's wine production region par excellence since the historical eruptions of Timanfaya in 1730, is a superb example of the success of sustainability.

After seeing how the devastating force of the volcanoes destroyed many villages and important farmlands on an island which already had few agricultural resources, Lanzarote's people came together and in a collective effort of triumph over adversity;

they put their skills to use and together with hard work and ingenuity found a way to make the volcanic ash work in their favour, in a way that would result in an increase in agricultural and economic yield for the islanders. Lanzarote wine is literally fruit of the volcano because the traditional farming technique uses the volcanic ash in a skilled way to plant the grapevine and maintains a total respect for natural balance.

Despite being declared a Natural Protected Landscape, La Geria, is in actual fact a landscape that has been greatly shaped by man, and in this sense it is an artificial landscape. For more than three centuries, thousands of hands have transformed its hundreds of hectares for farming. La Geria is also a landscape marked by suffering in the sense that it has been built from the efforts and continuous sacrifice of generations of poor farmers who have worked within the constraints of a rigid social system. Metre by metre, simple farmers or small or larger property owners altered the appearance of the land to reap the maximum benefit. They did so, however, following sustainable principles, even before the term was coined, because the peasant farmers of the island instinctively knew that the best way to ensure their survival was to adapt to their natural surroundings without overexploiting them.

Treatment with sulphur is essential to prevent pests in ecological and sustainable farming.

Ecological Viticulture

Ecological viticulture not only means obtaining healthier grapes but it also has many benefits for the biodiversity of the environment and for the health of the viticulturists themselves. This method of grape growing has increased in recent years and is being applied to all aspects of plant treatment in Lanzarote. In 2009 only 4 hectares of land were certified as ecological and just one winery, that of Bodegas Los Bermejos. However, by 2013 two more wineries were certified; Vega de Yuco and El Grifo which together harvested nearly 60,000 kilograms of grapes, the equivalent of approximately 3% of the island's total production.

For several years a greater awareness of treatments with pesticides has been raised thanks to regular courses run by the island's authorities and by the Regulatory Board as well as advice offered by the wineries' technical teams. The vineyards at El Grifo use an integrated production method and, being one of the few vineyards in the Canaries with this certification it also offers its viticulturists as consultants on this pest control method. Integrated production means giving priority to traditional ecological treatments and allows other types of treatments only in certain exceptional circumstances.

Although the wine making process is ecological in the majority of the island's wineries, there are three wineries with wines that have been certified as being made with organic grapes; Bodegas El Grifo and Bodegas Vega de Yuco have one wine each whilst Bodegas Los Bermejos, pioneers in making organic wine since 2002, make 3 different organic wines, a dry Malvasia, a dry Diego and a rosé made with Listán Negra grapes.

Cultivation Regions

There are two main regions on the island where grapevines are cultivated:

- The first and the most distinctive is composed of the areas of **La Geria**, **Masdache** and **Tinajo**. The region covers practically the whole area from the Monumento al Campesino monument in Mozaga stretching down to Uga and bordering Timanfaya National Park on the west and the San Bartolomé and Tinajo main road to the east.

- The second area of grapevines can be found growing in the north of the island in an area known as **Ye-Lajares**.

La Geria: Is a grape growing region situated between the municipal districts of Yaiza and Tías. Owing to the sheer density of the layer of volcanic lapilli or *rofe*, which can reach as far as 3 metres deep in places, a system of craters or pits is used in La Geria. As each pit occupies considerable space, crop density is somewhat lower than in other regions of the island where different methods are used. It is not the largest grape-growing region, but it is the most distinctive and is home to the majority of wineries that are open to the public. In fact it was in this region where this unique means of growing grapevines was first discovered after the three years of volcanic eruptions between 1730-1736, and then it was later extended to the rest of the island.

Masdache - Tinajo: Is the largest region divided into two sub-areas: Tinajo where the cultivation system is in walled trenches and in Masdache itself which has extensive fields of vineyards. The depth of the pits here is not as deep as in La Geria and therefore there is greater planting density. There are two wineries of note open to the public in this region; Bodegas El Grifo and its Wine Museum and Bodegas Los Bermejos.

Ye - Lajares: This area is located between the two municipal districts of Haría and Teguise. It is a low productivity region owing to the area's soil type. Harvesting here starts earlier than elsewhere, at the beginning of July.
The areas of La Geria, Tinajo and Masdache are protected by the Protected Landscape of La Geria Special Plan approved in 2013 and comprise 5,200 hectares which extend from Mozaga to Uga.

Deep pits in La Geria. Some of these pits can reach as far as 3 metres deep and measure 10 metres in diameter. They can usually be found where large amounts of *rofe* accumulate on the mountain sides.

Grapevines planted in rows in the Masdache region. This system is possible with a thinner layer of *rofe*, enabling a larger quantity of grapevines to be planted.

CULTIVATION REGIONS IN LANZAROTE

Wineries, or *Bodegas*

There are 18 wineries that come under the auspices of the *Consejo Regulador*, or Regulatory Board body of *Denominación de Origen* Lanzarote wines and they can be found in different regions throughout the island. Out of these 18 wineries, 14 are located in the La Geria - Masdache - Tinajo area. The Regulatory Board for the Designation of Origin (D.O) 'Lanzarote Wines' was created in 1993. It brings together 18 wineries, more than 1,700 viticulturists and represents 2,000 hectares of vineyards on the island of Lanzarote. The remit of the this Regulating Board includes promoting

the wines, as well as implementing quality control which is reflected by the certified labels on the bottles of wine produced on the island.

The wineries do not only depend on the yield from their own vineyards, they also purchase the harvest of small viticulturists which means that the grapes that go into making their wines could belong to any number of small growers. This peculiarity means that the big wine producers maintain close links to the small growers and also carry out consultancy work.

3. HISTORY OF WINE IN LANZAROTE

by Juan José Otamendi

Although Lanzarote was the first island of the Archipelago to be occupied by the Europeans (1402), it was the last to actually produce wine. It might be some consolation, however, to know that the first wine documented on the islands was wine brought to Lanzarote by the conquerors in their expedition. According to the 'Le Canarien' chronicle, there were thirty six barrels of wine (probably to consume and to trade with) which was only enough to last until the end of that year.

Perhaps the first wine to be produced on the Archipelago was in Fuerteventura in the first decade of the 15th century with grapes from 'the vines of Aníbal', the bastard son of French knight and explorer, Gadifer. In the last quarter of that century the islands not yet belonging to the Crown of Castile (Gran Canaria, Tenerife and La Palma) started to produce wines, initially just for local consumption but with the discovery of America, production soon expanded to supply the fleets, a market that had previously been monopolised by Andalusian wine. The growth of the wine trade was unstoppable until it became the most important area of trade. It was thanks to the luxury 'Canary' wine produced in the second half of the 16th century, that Canarian wines became most prestigious, competing with the wines of Jerez and gracing the best tables in Europe. Indeed, Shakespeare made mention of both wines.

Lanzarote, however, was still awaiting the chance to make its own wines; very probably an attempt was made to grow grape vines but it befell the same fate as grapes in the Caribbean, in that the environmental conditions were not favourable enough to support their cultivation. During the 17th century, wine consumed on Lanzarote would have been brought from the larger Canary Islands and from Madeira. Wine import duties were the main source of income for the Island Council at that time and it would have needed to use its limited funds on maintaining the water deposit reservoirs which held the rainwater for use by the local population as well as animals.

This was the case, at least, until the eruptions of 1730-1736. It is well documented in a memo from the Lanzarote *Cabildo*, Island Council, numbered 18/XII/1834 that was written retrospectively: "*Before the cited period of 1730 in the northern and easterly parts of the island, which they called the 'upper volcano', there were fruit trees like fig trees, peach trees, almond trees, olive trees, plum trees, palm trees and vines which despite providing good fruit failed to supply enough to meet needs, but after the volcanic eruptions in the aforementioned year, 1730 and up till 1737, crops were planted and seeds were sown... and in the region of the 'lower volcano' they planted many vines, digging pits in the volcanic sands until they reached the primitive soil... from the very volcanoes they made stone houses, water*

23

Image by Teodoro Maisch (1927) provided by kind permission of the Lanzarote Island Council's Historical Heritage Service.

deposits, walls and shelters... and they even planted in the fissures which had opened up in the crumbly volcanoes... managing to produce abundant crops of must for local consumption with enough to export to the Americas once made into liquor; it turned out to be a source of wealth."

Indeed, even before the eruptions came to an end, farmers realised that if they removed the volcanic ash where it wasn't too deep to do so, they could plant trees and vines and they would soon flourish. The blanket of volcanic ash made what was previously impossible, possible. The effects of the extremely scarce rainfall and the relentless wind (which not only makes it difficult for the plant to grow but also dries out the soil) were alleviated thanks to this blanket of *picón* or volcanic ash. Calling it *picón* was a small play on words as this was the name given to minute pieces of coal that were commercially available until a couple of decades ago, especially in Andalusia, which was similar in appearance - whilst not particularly funny, the nickname did catch on.

A further difficulty was, and still is, the wind that makes growing plants extremely difficult or prevents it all together, the exception being robust fig trees or mulberry bushes which withstand the constant trade winds well. The agrarian technology to combat this was well known in the Azores, especially on the island of Pico, where from the second half of the 16th century they had started to protect the plants with walls made of the rock from the petrified volcanic lava flow.

Providing protection from the wind in this way means the grapevines have to be low growing, extending close to the ground rather than growing upwards. Subsequently each vine occupies a great deal of space which means that inevitably there is a low density of crop plantation per hectare. The

Image taken in the 1950s by Martín Arteta shared with the *Memoria de Lanzarote* historical archive (www.memoriadelanzarote.com) courtesy of Arminda Arteta.

maximum possible attempted in any one plot of land in Lanzarote is of 900 plants, but the number normally varies between 400 and 600. In areas where the layer of volcanic ash is thick, the pits have to be larger, therefore reducing the number of plants to 300.

Both circumstances, which remain unchanged today, mean growers are left with no option other than implementing what is often labelled as an 'extreme' method of viticulture. As internationally renowned scholar Huetz de Lemps describes in his work *Vignobles et vins d'Espagne; L'étonant vignoble de Lanzarote.* - ('The Vineyards of Spain - the astonishing vineyard of Lanzarote'). When Huetz decided to publish another piece of work on extreme viticulture entitled *Les Vins de l'impossible* ('Impossible Wines') he chose an image of a Lanzarote vineyard to grace the cover.

There are many notarised documents from the mid 18th century which attest to the hollowing out of pits in the volcanic sand, that is to say digging away the small volcanic pebbles to allow the planting of vines or fruit trees in the soil below.

The dramatic proliferation of vineyards can be explained for the most part by the merchants of Tenerife who encouraged cultivation in Lanzarote, much as they had in La Gomera and El Hierro, other islands run by feudal lords. Their encouragement was driven by the need to acquire liquor not only for export to America but also to fortify their own wines as they had started to produce stronger more alcoholic coloured wines, much like the Madeiras of that time. The Tenerife merchants' taste for Lanzarote's liquors was also prompted by financial motives, as importing liquors from the Spanish mainland became subject to hefty tax levies.

George Glas, a Scottish merchant and expert on Canarian society in the latter part of the 18th century, was a wine merchant and regular visitor to Lanzarote. In his 'Description of the Canary Islands' he recounts how vineyards came about in Lanzarote; his impressions can be dated back to the beginning of the 1760s, some twenty five years after the end of the eruptions. "Up until 30 years ago Lanzarote did not produce wine. But then a volcano erupted which covered many fields with dust and small pumice stone pebbles which have improved the soil to such an extent that now there are vines planted there which flourish and produce grapes, but the wine is weak, of poor quality and so bitter that a foreigner would not be able to taste the difference between this wine and vinegar, it is, however, very healthy." He then clarifies, "The volcanoes that started in 1730 did not stop their spewing until 1735. They hurled such a vast quantity of volcanic ash across the land that it was left exceedingly well fertilised. So, since then the islanders have

Lanzarote under the Volcano by José de León Hernández

A few years ago, archaeologist and Doctor of History, José de León Hernández, published the book, Lanzarote under the Volcano. His prolific and thorough research builds a picture of the history and geography of the Lanzarote which remained buried under lava after the Timanfaya eruptions in the 18th century. The author explains the motivation for writing his book:

"...it was to try and make islanders and the millions of visitors to the island ask themselves about what once lay under that immense sea of lava and volcanic ash before the eruptions in the 18th century. Providing an answer to this question was the main aim of the book. Many eyes look and have looked over that vast territory in many very different ways. (...) Everyone has observed how in the ordinary way of things this territory measures more than 200 square kilometres (almost the same area as the island of El Hierro) and see its protective carapace made of stones and ash, imagining it as a bottomless landscape, a part of the island with no history, no past, in other words, with no people.

The question is what happened during the more than one thousand five hundred years that land was occupied by the original inhabitants, the Majos? What villages did they populate? What constructions did they build? What cultural heritage did they leave behind there? What happened in that area, one of the most appreciated on the island? And the eruptions? What happened to the chapels, houses, farmyards, flour mills, water deposits, water wells.... that once stood in their thousands on the planes and hillsides, coasts and badlands? What became of those people who lost everything? Where did they go and live, cultivate the land, shepherd? What influence did all of this have on the reorganisation of the new island that emerged when the earth stopped burning? Can we talk of a before and after in the history of Lanzarote?"

The passion behind the research is palpable and it makes for recommended reading. It also provides key insights into an essential chapter in the evolution of the landscape and the society of the island of Lanzarote.

Historical Sources

A diverse range of books is available to study the history of Lanzarote and although there are still great gaps that need to be filled, there are generic texts or more specialist books about specific aspects of Lanzarote's history. For those who want a more in-depth study of the island's history in general, we recommend the collection entitled *Jornadas de Estudios de Lanzarote y Fuerteventura*. They comprise thirteen volumes compiled by various specialists and are the main collection of scientific study about both islands. In the field of agriculture and the world of wine production there are various works worth pointing out. Researchers Jaime Gil and Marta Peña have written about different aspects of Lanzarote's agriculture like grains and herbs. Juan José Otamendi has published various texts about the history of wine, including *La Tonelería tradicional y los vinos de Canarias* ('Traditional cooperage and wines of the Canaries') and he coordinates the library in the Wine Museum in the La Geria, which is one of the best of its kind in the Canaries and, indeed, Spain.

With the arrival of the digital world new platforms are being created on the Internet all the time. It is especially worth visiting the historical archive *Memoriadelanzarote.com* which has collated thousands of images, texts, audiovisual records, historical news items and documentary heritage of the island. It is also worth consulting the digital archive of the University of Las Palmas in Gran Canaria (*Memoria Digital de Canarias de la ULPGC*) and the portal of old photographs in the Canaries collated by FEDAC.

planted plenty of fruit trees and grapevines which have taken very well; even though the wine they produce is bitter and weak and is only any good for making liquor."

On account of their trade in liquor, the merchants of Tenerife established themselves in Arrecife and financed the cultivation of vineyards in exchange for must which they distilled in their 'offices' or rudimentary distilleries. In this way, they contributed to the growth of what was to become the future capital of the island. As Montelongo and Falero observed in their book *El Puerto de Arrecife* ('The Port of Arrecife'), it was the opening of distilleries and wineries in the port of Arrecife that gave this city its economic kick-start and not the soda ash industry which is usually credited with giving the city its economic heyday. Although it is not surprising that the urban boom in Arrecife has been attributed to this product, strictly speaking, it merely propelled forward what the wine industry had already put in motion.

The second half of the 18th century was Records of agreements made between the two Island Councils (Cabildos) reveal that consumption of these wines began on Lanzarote and Fuerteventura in the second half of the 18th century. However, it was not until almost the turn of the century that Arrecife's distilleries and wine trade finally passed into Lanzarote hands.

Wine production was never the most important contributor to the island's economy, but it was a useful reserve asset. In fact, as a result of the temporary wealth that the soda ash industry and later the trade in cochineal brought a few islanders, investment was made in the wine industry which resulted in 'modern' constructions such as wineries being built. According to statistics compiled by the Marquis of Tabalosos, and recovered by historian Rumeu de Armas, 1775 saw the production of 4,500 barrels, some 2,160,000

1970s postcard provided by kind permission of Rafael Silva.

litres (3 million kilos of grapes) and this was despite the fact that as reported in the *el Compendio* at the time, a fourth of the vines had not yet yielded fruit as they had only recently been planted. Therefore it was not long, before wine production in Lanzarote surpassed that of Gran Canaria and La Palma. Wines and liquors were exported from Lanzarote to the other islands and then sent on to America and the Thirteen Colonies, the birthplace of the United States.

Wine production was regarded as a reserve asset within the realm of the island's agricultural production up until the end of the 19th century. Although there were some large vineyards and big wineries, grape growing was generally quite widespread and it would have been unusual for a family not to have its own grapevines. Until the 1970s owning vines meant producing your own wine for private consumption and only occasionally, if there was enough left over in a given year would it have been sold.

Whilst Listán was initially the grape of preference as it bore the most fruit, as the 19th century progressed, what had been considered traditionally Canarian varieties, especially the Malvasía (also the Diego and the Muscat) went from strength to strength in Lanzarote but declined in other wine growing islands like Tenerife. We are aware of this phenomenon thanks to reports compiled at the 1877 National Viticulture and Wine Making Exhibition by the engineer, José Barrioso. It is surprising that this choice of variety and the types of wine produced would coincide with the traditional ones of the Archipelago that date from the second half of the 16th century, a choice changed before the powdery mildew blight which struck the rest of the islands in 1853. The Malvasía grape which had all but disappeared according to Viera and Clavijo, some eighty years prior to the observations of Barrioso, was well established in Lanzarote.

In the 1870s, the British Consular Reports coincided with the findings of French doctor and naturalist Vernau, who pointed out that the vegetation was very poor, stating:

"*However, among the plants that have been introduced there is one that prospers and that is the vine. It produces a white wine between 12% and 14% in strength which is very pleasant to the taste and also has the advantage of being very cheap. In conclusion, the white wines of Lanzarote that are only 11% or 12% could pass as great wines. The ordinary red wines of Gran Canaria when they have not been fortified, are between 12% and 14%. These, like the Lanzarote wines cost about 25 francs per hectolitre.*"

The Malvasía wine referred to in the reports probably resembles today's wines more closely than those made in the first seven decades of the 20th century which had a higher alcohol level due to extended ripening of the grape and were cloudier due to using a mixture of grape varieties. Canarian wines, especially from Tenerife which dominated and continues to dominate in terms of quantity of grape production, lost their international acclaim and reverted to the safety of the domestic market for local consumption and supplying boats.

The last decade of the 19th century and the first three of the 20th brought important technological breakthroughs in the shape of strong cement tanks which partially replaced wooden containers; so too came transfer pumps and hydraulic presses which pretty well totally dispensed with beam presses, the new de-stemmers replaced the old separators and then came early mechanized attempts at bottling.

By 1930, there were twelve wine establishments in the port of Arrecife. They generally belonged to winery owners and their purpose was two-pronged; to sell wine to the public and also to use for storage before shipping overseas. Thanks to the early road system, the wineries would make use of carts pulled by mules to transport a precious cargo of two barrels of wine.

The birth of the tourist industry in the 1960s and 1970s spelled the end for many traditional wineries. Camels were also affected; once essential to Lanzarote's viticulture to transport the grape harvest, the must and the wine, they ceased to be part of the island's agricultural tradition and were reassigned roles in the tourist sector. Luckily, Lanzarote no longer depended on an agriculture that revolved around harsh conditions and uncertainty because of the scarce rainfall. Some large landowners (on a Lanzarote scale) came together under the chairmanship of Doctor Bethencourt and set up Montaña Clara S.A. in order to make wine together and build a brand new winery. With a few exceptions, the majority of other wineries started closing down. Private growers would start to offer their grapes to the wineries and bit by bit small private wine makers would give up completely.

Another technological revolution took place in the early 1980s with the introduction of stainless steel and refrigeration equipment which was pioneering in the Archipelago. This was mainly at the behest of oenologist Felipe Blanco Pinilla who introduced changes to Lanzarote wines to make them more closely resemble those produced in the second half of the 19th century. Not only did he have a hand in transforming Lanzarote wines, but he also went on to revolutionize Tenerife wines as director of Viña Norte wineries.

The Lanzarote Regulatory Board (D.O) to certify the origin and quality of Lanzarote's wines came into effect in the 1990s and its first priority, like other appellation boards, was to demand discipline in grape growing and wine making. Having achieved this aim, it has focussed this century on helping wine growers and in raising public awareness of the symbolic importance of this crop. This

Picture of the pits in La Geria without their traditional protective crescent walls.

favourable trend has enabled new wineries to break into the sector (a list of which can be found on the D.O. Lanzarote website) with excellent quality, carefully produced wines which have been well received by consumers and which respect the nuances of viticulture.

A third of Lanzarote's vineyards have been lost in the last few years alone. The contributory factors being, as world experts unanimously acknowledge, that they have to survive in extreme conditions, the average yield is ten times smaller than in other wine growing regions and the harvest is unpredictable with huge swings due to the irregular rainfall. From an economic perspective, the wine industry is relatively insignificant as the total value of the grape from one year to the next does not exceed three or four million Euros. The reality is that it actually provides more assets for the tourist sector than for the wine industry itself. It is essential, therefore, that rather than directing European environment funds to the great majority of crops grown under plastic, like bananas, they should be diverted to viticulturists instead. It would also be of enormous benefit for the region if the politicians, no matter what their party, could work together to find a definitive solution to the long-running saga of the rural planning scheme for La Geria - it is a perfect example of a futile endeavour that sees the wineries handcuffed by regulations that are imposed upon them in order to conform to code but which actually stand in the way of the business of making excellent wines.

Lanzarote vineyards represent the skeletal remains of the island's agricultural industry which has all but disappeared. To ensure their survival, Lanzarote's wines need to stand proudly among the best wines in Spain for their capacity to show how the grape rewards the viticulturists for their hard work and effort. The situation is precarious but we should be optimistic. It remains to be seen.

Farmer loading large baskets onto a camel during the grape harvest. Photograph taken in the 1950s offered to www.memorialanzarote.com by kind permission of Antonio Lorenzo.

The Camel

The camel (*camelus dromedarius*) arrived on Lanzarote from Africa in 1404 together with the first Moors. Chroniclers relate how camels used to swim over, tied to the boats; their agility and buoyancy helping them to survive and fend off occasional attacks from fish.

In 1730 there were 5,000 inhabitants on the island and 1,700 camels. During the historic eruptions of Timanfaya many camels were transported to La Graciosa because they were prone to die of asphyxiation, according to specialist Francisco J. Fabelo.

They became the perfect agricultural tool and were not only useful in La Geria but also in other types of farming. They were the beasts of burden that could carry the heaviest loads and proved ideal for pulling a plough, for sowing seeds and for carrying out other heavy tasks. Farmers on Lanzarote used to always use camels up until a few decades ago. In the 1940s there

were 3,000 camels on the island. There are two types of camel on Lanzarote, the *moro*, from Africa and the Canarian or *canario* (also known as the *majorero*) from Fuerteventura, which is not as tall but is stockier.

Camels are mainly found in the tourist sector these days and are rarely used for farming. This came about in the 1950s when camels were used to carry the first travellers on trips around Timanfaya. Nowadays, the majority of camels are based in Uga and traipse to Timanfaya every day where they spend all day taking visitors on rides up the slope of a volcano.

Those interested in seeing camels carrying out their age-old traditional roles can do so in La Geria during the festival of the grape harvest which is held every year on 15th August. If you wish to enjoy the sights from high up on camel back, it is possible to do so in Timanfaya and in La Geria.

Camel loaded up with dried corn stalks and other dried crops (used for animal fodder) in Masdache. Photograph taken in the 1950s courtesy of Antonio Lorenzo.

Tribute to the camel with a plough

by Agustín Espinosa from his book *Lancelot 28º -7º* (published by Ediciones Alfa, Madrid, 1929)

For you - camel with a plough of Lanzarote - I give my specifically military salute. For your slow strides like those of a retired general. For your gestures of one misunderstood. For your great wooden sabre, above all. For that great sabre plough which you know how to pull with such comic grace through the flat earth of Lanzarote, as if through the carpets of a grand consular drawing room. With such a sad grace that only Charlie Chaplin could call you his master.

How beautiful you are, camel of Lanzarote! You, who without a plough is the ugliest of all creatures. Because you are ugly and in you, your nudity is more noticeable than in any other beast.

I shall always remember - camel with plough of Lanzarote - the first impression of your

ploughing silhouette like that of a great figure on the Steppe. I shall always remember smiling at your great film for minorities (Chaplin is the only other to have made me smile so). If you were to go to New York - camel with plough of Lanzarote - you would find a backer for your films. You would work with Buster Keaton and with Mary Pickford, with Charlie Chaplin and with Harold. And you would have your audience of children who would applaud you loudly as you won battles and seized castles with your great wooden sabre.

For you - camel with plough of Lanzarote - my specifically military salute. And my salute - also - as a jolly spectator of your great new art form. Of your unappreciated art - camel for minorities: master of the actors of transformation.

4. LA GERIA, WINE LANDSCAPE

Francisco de León is one of the island's 'true warriors' as illustrator and painter Santiago Alemán would say. For he has worked for decades in La Geria and at eighty years old still does so on virtually a daily basis. As a young boy he started to dig pits and build stone wind breaks. He used to work from dawn until dusk shovelling the *picón* gravel to create the hollows. Generations of Franciscos have transformed the face of thousands of hectares of land in a sustainable way, in a totally manual process which began in the 18th century and which is seeking a means to endure long into the 21st century.

Those who consume Lanzarote wines should know that with their money they are also helping to conserve a landscape that is natural but at the same time man-made, one that is unique in the world. The magic of La Geria lies not only in its stunning scenery. Its visual impact and beauty combine with outstanding ethnographic and environmental features derived of the Herculean efforts carried out by thousands of anonymous farm workers who laboured under extremely precarious and harsh conditions with exemplary results. La Geria is the embodiment of respect for and symbiosis with nature. La Geria is a landscape full of visual beauty but also one steeped in social, cultural and ecological lessons to be learnt.

Public institutions, private organisations and individuals are currently making new efforts to keep the fragile and delicate territory of La Geria alive. The central axis around which everything revolves in this unique micro cosmos, is wine. Therefore, all the efforts being made to prevent La Geria from disappearing are focussed on revitalising the region's viticulture. With the arrival of tourism, Lanzarote underwent a sociological and economic transformation which left the veteran farmer with no one to take up the reins. This phenomenon has led to a gradual and alarming process of abandonment in La Geria and other regions. Modernisation of the island deprived the countryside of new generations of farmers because the vast majority of young people who would have been the next generation of farmers moved to the service sector instead.

Now, many are looking to wine and wine tourism as a means of guaranteeing the future of a totally unique landscape that is brimming with culture, biodiversity, ecology and provides the setting for stories of dedication on the part of thousands of anonymous heroes just like Francisco. In reality, Lanzarote's farm workers were pioneers in the formula that the planet is crying out for in the 21st century: a pact of sustainability between man and the earth's natural resources. This is the true value of Lanzarote wines.

Photograph by Nicolás Melián.

Francisco de León.

Place Names
by Agustín Pallarés

La Geria is a vast territory which opens up like a wide valley between the Chupadero and Diama mountains on the northern side and Mounts Tinasoria, Guardilama and Caldera Gaida to the south. It starts a few kilometres northeast of Uga and covers an area of some 3 kms in this same direction towards Mount Peña Palomas.

This landscape is characterized by the thick layer of lapilli or black volcanic ash which covers most of the terrain. It is generally 2 m deep but it is twice that in the area northeast of Montaña Diama in the place known as 'El Cañón'. This double layer of ash was created by the first volcano to erupt in 1730, the Caldera de los Cuervos, and then on top of that fell the second layer caused by the eruption of the Caldera de la Rilla which threw out the largest quantity of volcanic material and affected a much larger area of land.

Old files reveal interesting historical information about the region to the effect that, in 1571, the married couples Marcos Verde and Justa Melián and Diego Vázquez and Margarita Ruiz sold their lands to the Lanzarote priest Luis de Bethencourt, naming:

"Our property and estate in La Geria, and land from the wall inwards which are already prepared and those yet to be worked." Among the buildings listed in that estate were; *"houses, flour mills, water collection reservoirs that were in use and ready to be used and a water tank."*

These were properties which would seem to have encompassed large areas of land. It is particularly interesting to note the reference to the 'wall', which according to this document, surrounded these aforementioned properties because it could give an indication as to the

origin of the name of the region, as a few kilometres to the east of Tahíche stands the La Geria wall which is particularly notable for its size, measuring approximately 1 km in length and a little less in width.

There are other theories as to the origin of the name. One possibility is that *geria* could be of Berber origin. However, there is a place of the same name in the province of Valladolid and in Castilian Spanish there is also the word 'heria' pronounced with an aspirated 'h' which is an archaic form of 'feria', which is still in use in Mexico. According to Sabino Berthelot (1842/1978:160) it might originate from the Berber term 'yeria' which means 'grain'. It has also been mooted that La Geria received its name from the semicircular windbreaks that protect the grapevines, but this would seem an assumption based on no actual evidence given that these walls were not built until after the area was covered by volcanic ash in 1730. Another reason for ruling this possibility out is the fact that, as the documents indicate, the name 'La Geria' dates back to at least the 16th century. Furthermore, these stone windbreaks are more commonly referred to as *abrigos*, or 'shelters', although there are members of the older generations who refer to them as *goire*.

In the first decade of the 18th century, the Church's incumbent of the time, Diego de Laguna, became the owner of an estate in La Geria which had water deposit reservoirs and various outhouses and it was he that ordered the construction of the La Caridad chapel.

A. de la Hoz (1962:237), who was a landowner in La Geria, together with the previously mentioned incumbent and the bishop of the diocese of the Canaries at the time, Pedro Dávila y Cárdenas, recounts that when the bishop found out that volcanic ash had fallen on his property being unaware of the magnitude of the disaster, naively gave the order that all the ash that had rained down on his lands should be removed and

35

Work is traditionally carried out barefoot in the pit.

carried away by camels. When it was realised that such a task was impossible as La Hoz explained, they dug out some pits to reach down to the top soil and planted linseed plants and pumpkins which subsequently produced great fruit.

A document filed in the Simancas archive dated 19th December 1730, stated that there were seven residents in La Geria. Indeed, according to a later report on Lanzarote compiled by engineer, José Ruiz Cermeño when he visited the island in 1772, there were seven families living in this area of La Geria and the *Compendio brebe y famosso* report of 1776 came up with the same number.

In his dictionary (1850/1986:116), P. Madoz says that over a five-year period La Geria produced; *"Apart from fruit from various different trees, mostly fig trees, 1,500 barrels of superior quality must to make*

liquor that was exported to America where it is held in great esteem."

Around the same dates according to the document *Yaiza and its Land* volume II 1999:47 in La Geria there was; *'one two-storey house, 4 houses and 6 huts which together gave shelter to 30 souls.'* By 1877, the number of residents had increased considerably and was home to 85 inhabitants who all cultivated grapes. Conversely, according to P. de Olive, (1860) there were just five houses and six huts.

La Geria has been declared a Natural Protected Space, a status awarded in recognition of its unique landscape where the land is dominated by intense black due to the thick layer of lapilli, dotted with many pits where, in the summer, the green branches of the grape vine can be seen creeping over the top, creating a colour contrast that is unique to any grape growing region in the world.

A viticulturist whilst harvesting the Listán Negra grape. She is wearing the typical farm worker's hat.

5. NATURAL ELEMENTS

Climate

The Canary Islands are volcanic in origin and belong to the natural region known as Macaronesia, together with the Atlantic archipelagos of Cape Verde, the Azores, Madeira and the Savage (Selvagens) Islands. The Canaries enjoy a dry tropical humid climate but their location in the Atlantic and the terrain relief of some islands mean there are many topoclimates. The archipelago is dominated by the trade winds generated by the anticyclone, or high pressure area of the Azores. The islands' proximity to the Sahara desert also affects the climate as it brings occasional spates of very warm dry air carrying large quantities of dust suspended in the air called *calima*. The combination of winds, ocean currents and pressure systems make the temperatures in the Canaries remarkably stable and not too hot. These characteristics have given rise to great biological diversity, which together with the landscape and geological richness, make for the existence of four National Parks in the Canaries and some of the islands being designated Unesco Biosphere Reserves with others having areas which have been declared World Heritage Sites.

Water and temperature

According to Lang's Rain Factor index, Lanzarote has a desert climate, whilst Martonne's aridity index classifies it as hyper-arid and according to the Papadakis classification, it is a Mediterranean semi-arid subtropical climate.

The average annual rainfall is 110 litres per square metre, making it neither abundant nor regular. The dry season falls in the summer although there may be some rain due to humidity generated by the trade winds.

According to the Thornthwaite classification, the atmosphere around the Protected Landscape of La Geria is defined as arid and mesothermal with average annual temperatures that are mild and constant. While temperatures may not vary too greatly from a year-round perspective, there is a substantial variation between daytime and night-time temperatures in winter and summer months. Rainfall is very low and inconsistent qauntities fall at irregular intervals throughout the year, whilst never exceeding 200 mm per year.

The average year-round temperature is 20°. Temperatures are at their highest in August and coldest in January with an average annual fluctuation of 7.7° which clearly indicates the isothermal process brought about by the trade winds all year round. Top temperatures can exceed 40° which is because of air advection from the Sahara whilst lowest temperatures rarely drop lower than 10° in the winter months.

Crops and volcanoes

The whole of La Geria is covered with two distinct types of volcanic debris produced by the volcanic eruptions that took place in the 18th century. There are outflows of volcanic ash and lava as well as airborne pyroclasts, or tephra fragments. The outflows are either the aa-type jagged, 'badlands', with a rough clinkery surface or the pahoehoe lava flows which generally have a billowy, smoother surface. Pyroclasts can take the form of scoria, lapilli or ash; their size depending on how broken up they are. There is also another type of surface, the *kipuka*, or rises of land, which predate the eruptions and were not covered by lava.

Within the Protected Landscape of La Geria there are two types of soil substratum which relate to two distinct cultivation methods; the traditional system of planting in pits in soil found buried under layers of volcanic ash caused by the eruptions between 1730 - 36; and alternatively the *enarenado* or artificial sand pits which use soil from quarries located further afield, outside the boundaries of the Protected Space.

Soils

Lanzarote is born of basalt rock that dates back to the Middle and Late Pleistocene periods. It was subsequently combined with the lava flows from the island's historic eruptions and a layer of vegetation which, whilst sparse, is replete with important endemic species.

Another factor that lends the soil in La Geria its unique quality is the fact that it was buried under layers of volcanic ash that resulted from the eruptions in the 18th century. The soil buried under the lava is Paleorthid and Caciorthid, evolved from Series II material with similar characteristics to those of the cliffs of Famara and the mountain range of Los Ajaches. In farmed areas the soil is reddish in colour and clay-limey with a good average content of organic material which ensures a supply of nitrogen that is just right for grape vines. There are optimum quantities of the main macro nutrients (N, P, K) and the presence of free carbonates produce a basic PH.

Fauna

a) Invertebrates: especially insects such as arachnids and coleopterons and in particular, cave dwelling beetles and weevils. In the lava environment different species of springtails (collembola) flourish as well as arachnids and two species of grasshopper. There are also dragon flies, although these are summer visitors linked to weather systems brought by the Sahara.

b) Reptiles: there are three species found on Lanzarote; the Atlantic lizard, the East Canary Gecko and the smooth Majorero Gecko (this latter one needs confirmation but there is evidence of its presence in areas of Mozaga and Conil).

Birdlife in La Geria and the Volcano Natural Park is protected under the auspices of the Special Protection Area (SPA). It was designated a special area of interest to safeguard threatened species such as the Bulwer's petrel, Scopili's shearwater and the Lesser short-toed lark which are found in the region. This European Union directive (79/409) ensures the conservation of their habitat and considerably limits any activity in this fragile Protected landscape.

c) Mammals: Apart from game species, mammals are represented by two interesting species such as the north African hedgehog and the Canarian shrew.

d) Birds: There is a range of birdlife; ranging from marine birds like Bulwer's Petrel to rock dwelling birds of prey, (like the common kestrel, Barbary falcon and common barn owl) the raven and the plain swift, to name but a few. La Geria is home to a remarkable wealth of wildlife and birdlife. Significant populations of kestrels and owls can also be found in this Protected territory.

In addition to these aforementioned groups, La Geria also provides an important habitat for communities of birds that thrive in dry areas with species such as the stone curlew, lesser short-toed lark, trumpeter finch and Berthelot's pipit and the community of crop birds like the hoopoe, southern grey shrike, common linnet, Spanish sparrow and collared dove.

e) Game: particularly rabbits and partridges and to a lesser extent the European turtle dove, the rock dove and the quail.

As regards endangered species, it must be said that the unfortunate dwindling numbers of populations is due to the disappearance in wildlife in general on the island. This is mainly due to the decline in agriculture, but exacerbated by the shortage of water troughs and water deposits and even the use of poisons by some farmers.

Flora

These oceanic islands are renowned for being home to a huge variety of plant life. The original colonizing plants have developed into new species that have evolved by means of natural differentiation which has enabled them to seek a foothold in vacant niches and habitats and thrive; the result being the unique rich flora which we can see throughout the Canarian archipelago today.

In general, Lanzarote possesses species of flora which have adapted to living in harsh conditions of drought, badlands and wind for most of the year. For this reason the only arboreal plants here are palm trees. The most typical plants found on the island are subtropical verode succulents, spurge shrubs and giant cactus.

As many as 295 different classes of plants have been identified in the La Geria region alone, belonging to 65 different families and together accounting for 45.6% of Lanzarote's flora. There are four main types of vegetation depending on the characteristics of the area:

a) Lichens: this group began colonizing the recent layer of substratum in Timanfaya. The most prevalent species on the petrified lava flow are pioneer species such as *Stereocaulon Vesuvianum*, crustose lichen like *Lecanora*,

41

Stereocaulon vesuvianum lichen

Mallow

An old abandoned vineyard in La Geria overrun by Mediterranean saltwort and tree tobacco plants.

fructiose and foliose lichen like *Ramalina* and *Xanthoria* and sunburst lichen.

b) Rock-growing vegetation: Among this community of flora we can find different ferns such as hare's foot fern (*Davallia canariensis*) or southern maidenhair fern (*Adiantum capilllus veneris*). Within this community there are instances of shrub layer vegetation such as the native

Canary Island sage (*Savia canariensis*) the evergreen shrub Hypericum grandifolia or Asparagus Nesiotes. Also visible in this habitat are the perennial verodes (*Greenovia aeonietea*) which are of great scientific importance as they are an endemic species.

c) Nitrophilous pastures and grasslands: there are various examples of woody grasslands dotted around different areas unaffected by the Timanfaya eruptions. You can find common thatching grass (*Hyparrhenia hirta*), buffel-grass (*Cenchrus ciliaris*) as well as sowbane (*Chenopodio muralis*) and mallow grass (*Malvetun parviflorae*). Whilst these grasses are not endemic species, they are of huge importance to the island's birdlife, together with other plant types such as the cliff dwelling thistle. Barillas such as the common ice plant (*Mesembryanthemum crystallinum*), the slenderleaf ice plant and various members of the Betoideae family (*Patellifolia patellaris*) like chard are also found here. They are ruderal species being the first to colonize disturbed land and thrive in the nitrogen rich soil.

d) Shrub lands: There are two communities, the spurge family of succulents (*Kleinio-Euphorbietea canariensis*) which mainly comprise balsamiferous spurge (*Euphorbia balsamifera*) and the prickle-leaved spurge (*Euphorbia regis-jubae*). These are most commonly found in areas where crops have been abandoned and often grow alongside the yellow-flowering *Nauplius intermedius* from the Asteriscus family. The second community of shrubs is the most prolific kind of substitute vegetation and includes the barbed wire bush and the Mediterranean saltwort (*Launaea arborescens schyzoginetum sericeae*) which grow abundantly in areas unaffected by the volcanic eruptions as they manage to take a foothold in any type of altered soil or abandoned farmlands, thanks to their high colonizing capacity.

Fruit-bearing trees
by Ignacio Romero

Living alongside the grapevine (*Vitis vinifera*), which reigns over La Geria, there are a number of other fruit trees which also have an important role to play in terms of their effect on the landscape and the food they produce. If you look carefully, you can see how many peek over the top of the pits whilst others prefer to remain hidden inside and can only be identified upon closer inspection.

The Common Fig is one such tree, typically bearing abundant fruit. Figs once formed an integral part of Lanzarote's traditional diet until the late 20th century and going back even further in time, it is highly likely that figs were also part of the staple diet of the ancient inhabitants of the Canary Islands. Although yet to be proven in Lanzarote, archaeological studies certainly show this to be true in Gran Canaria and Tenerife. The fruit of the fig tree was eaten fresh or also dried which is why you can still see today paved areas within farmsteads used as drying areas where the farmers would lay them out to dry in the sun after harvesting. Dried figs was such an essential foodstuff that even today islanders refer to figs simply as 'fruit' and to dried figs as 'dried fruit'.

Together with the grapevines and the fig trees, there are many other types of fruit bearing trees which you would not expect to find given the scarce rainfall on Lanzarote. The layer of volcanic ash has a natural mulching effect on the soil which enables farmers to grow fruit trees at this latitude and in the island's semi-arid climate conditions.

The fig tree (*Ficus carica*) Moraceae family

The fig tree is a small tree or bush, although in Lanzarote the lack of other trees makes the fig tree stand out and dominate the landscape. Because of the wind, it is quite stumpy but some specimens have been known to grow as high as 5 metres. It is present in different areas of the globe but is mainly found in Asia and in the Mediterranean. It is undemanding of its soil quality and can withstand extended dry spells. It is a deciduous tree and bears fruit twice a year; once in June, when it is referred to as 'San Juan Fruit' after the local festival of this name, and again in August.

There are many varieties of fig tree which can be identified by their fruit and the shape of the leaves. In Lanzarote we typically find the following varieties; La Gomera, Negra, Conchinchina, Blanca, Cota, Bicariña, Brevera etc.

Fig tree

Dried fig locally known as 'dried fruit'

Black Mulberry (*Morus nigra*)
Moraceae family
Medium sized deciduous tree of Asian origin and cultivated throughout the world for its edible and tasty fruit. The black mulberry fruit called locally *mora*, is a dark purple black in colour when it is fully ripe. Prior to ripening it is green then red.

Guava (*Psidium guajava*)
Myrtaceae family
A small tree from America cultivated in Lanzarote as it tolerates dry spells and intense heat very well. Its guava fruit are very tasty and rich in vitamin C.

Orange tree (*Citrus × sinensis*)
Rutaceae family
The orange tree is small in size and originates from Asia but has been cultivated all over the world for its fruit; the orange.

Lemon tree (*Citrus × limon*)
Rutaceae family
The lemon tree is a small evergreen native to Asia and cultivated throughout the world for its fruit; the lemon.

Prickly Pear / Barbary Fig
(*Opuntia ficus-indica*) Cacteceae family
The prickly pear is a cactus bush native to Central America which is cultivated in many semi-arid regions of the world. Its fruit goes by many names, including 'Barbary fig', 'cactus pear' and 'tuna', and is eaten fresh or dried in the same way as figs. When the stalks and leaves are tender they are chopped and given to sheep, goats and camels as fodder. It is grown on Lanzarote in large quantities in Guatiza and Mala where it is farmed for the parasitic cochineal beetle which lives on it. The beetle is carefully extracted from the plant (*Dactylopius coccus*) and dried in order to produce a natural dye which is exploited commercially.

Avocado (*Persea americana*)
Lauraceae family
The avocado is a large tree which originates from Central America. The wind and lack of water in La Geria mean that it does not grow to great sizes. Its fruit, the avocado, is high in natural fats and is very popular.

Other trees that can be found include pear trees, nectarine and peach trees, olive trees, almond trees, medlar trees and carob trees.

Fig trees in the La Geria region.

Cross section diagram of the planted vine stock

Pit method:

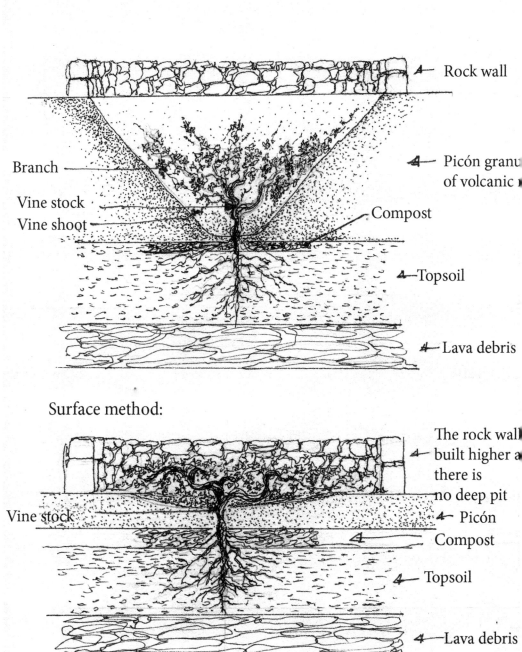

Rock wall

Branch

Picón granu
of volcanic i

Vine stock

Vine shoot

Compost

Topsoil

Lava debris

Surface method:

Vine stock

The rock wall
built higher a
there is
no deep pit

Picón

Compost

Topsoil

Lava debris

6. GRAPE CULTIVATION AND HARVESTING METHODS

Illustrations by Santiago Alemán

Various different methods are used to cultivate grapevines throughout Lanzarote including funnel-shaped pits, (*hoyos*), ditches (*zanjas*), vine arbours (*parrales*) and naturally formed fissures in the petrified lava flow (*chabocos*). The common element running through all these cultivation methods is *rofe*, or volcanic rock gravel, which provides a natural layer of insulation between the topsoil and the surface. It is so effective that it is not only used where it accumulated naturally after the eruptions, but also in artificial, dry-farmed crop beds. The layer of *rofe* varies in thickness depending on formations from earlier eruptions but is rarely less than 30 cms and can reach as much as 3 metres deep. The influence of the constant trade winds means that whatever the planting method, the vine will always be protected by a small wall of some kind, sheltering it from the winds blowing in from the north east. These walls, called *socos*, are built out of volcanic rock and are fixed in place using the dry stone wall method without the need for sealant or any other product to hold them together. The gaps between the rocks enable oxygen to flow freely around the plant. This gentle ventilation together with the insulating and moisture retention properties of the *rofe* combine to form a formidable defence against disease, drastically reducing the spread of fungal infection and pests.

The most distinctive cultivation method is the use of deep pits and it is these pits which shape the landscape in La Geria. They represent centuries of painstaking work and have been created over different periods of time since the volcanic eruptions; some even shelter grapevines that are hundreds of years old. The majority have been dug out manually, without the help of any machinery, meaning that Lanzarote's farmers have literally excavated each and every one by hand. The depth and diameter of the pit is dependent on how deep the layer of *picón* granules is and how far down the topsoil lies. Forming a semi-circle around each pit is a shelter of volcanic rocks called a *soco*. Cultivating grapes in these hand-dug pits only allows for low density planting resulting in low levels of production per hectare. It is estimated that 1,500 kilos of grapes are produced from an average 400 plants per hectare in the region of La Geria.

The very nature of these hand-dug pits, some dating back hundreds of years, and varying in depth depending on their location, means they are not arranged in a regular pattern. However, nowadays as vineyards are being renovated, machines are being used to reduce and even out the layers of *rofe*, a process which enables the pits to be laid out in a regular pattern and subsequently allows higher planting density.

1. Cultivation in pits (*hoyos*)

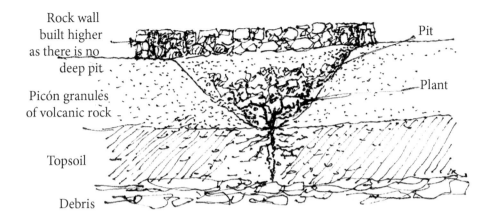

Rock wall built higher as there is no deep pit

Picón granules of volcanic rock

Topsoil

Debris

Pit

Plant

Cross section view of a pit. These pits are funnel-shaped and the vine sits inside. The different layers can be seen starting from the debris, or rubble from previous eruptions, the topsoil or fertile soil in which the vine is actually planted, the insulating layer of *rofe* on top of the pit and then the wall made out of volcanic rock. These walls are crescent-shaped and are positioned to buffer against the prevailing north easterly trade winds. The depth of the pit depends on the quantity of *rofe* that settled in a particular region - in some parts of La Geria it can be as much as 3 metres deep. The vine is planted in the fertile soil and is covered with *rofe* which has a mulching effect and retains moisture.

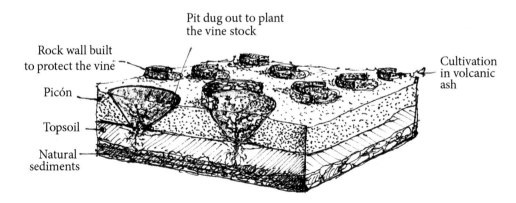

Pit dug out to plant the vine stock

Rock wall built to protect the vine

Picón

Topsoil

Natural sediments

Cultivation in volcanic ash

Cross section view of land planted using the pit method. As a consequence of being dug out by hand and positioned in a way that would make the most of the land, the pits would end up being laid out in an irregular pattern, rendering it impossible to access with any type of machinery.

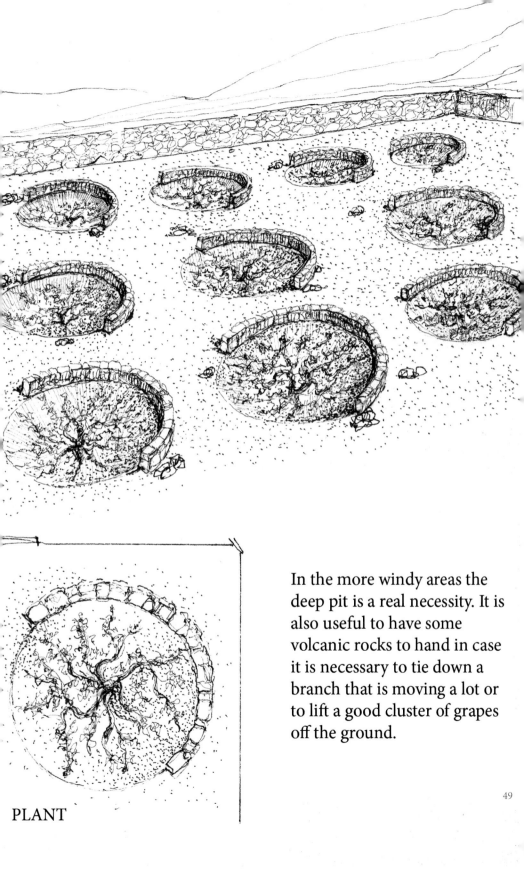

In the more windy areas the deep pit is a real necessity. It is also useful to have some volcanic rocks to hand in case it is necessary to tie down a branch that is moving a lot or to lift a good cluster of grapes off the ground.

PLANT

La Geria burns!

On occasion, visitors to La Geria will be greeted by the dramatic sight of patches of white smoke billowing out of the otherwise black landscape. Although reminiscent of geysers spurting from a bubbling volcano underfoot, it is in fact, smoke from smouldering fires burning off dead leaves and dried stalks. The layout of the pits make it difficult to access the vineyards and transport waste away, so the viticulturist is tasked with collecting dead cuttings from the pruning season in February (which coincides with the waning moon) piling them together ready for burning along with waste produced throughout the rest of the year, including the summer pruning which takes place after harvesting.

Nowadays, some of the waste is made into compost which goes back into the soil as natural fertiliser but it is still common practice to make these small fires, resulting in this curious spectacle.

Unlike other grape cultivation methods around the world, in Lanzarote, the vines are pruned in such a way as to train them parallel to the surface and no more than 20 cms high, so that they are protected from the wind thanks to the deep pit and sheltering wall.

2. Cultivation in Trenches

Growing grapes in trenches consists of planting vines in blocks of straight lines with stone walls running behind each trench and placed on either side, protecting them from the wind. Even though this method is not particularly common, it does mean that some of the farming can be done with the help of machinery. The layer of *rofe* is not as deep as in the pits so each one can be spaced closer together thus increasing density and producing yields as big as 3,000 kilos per hectare. Whilst some farms have parallel trenches covering the whole of their land, for the most part, they are normally placed in such a way that they border the edges of farmlands leaving the central area free for growing other crops such as cereals, potatoes and different vegetables.

Although not commonly used in La Geria, these rectangular trench-type pits are widespread in regions such as Masdache, Tinajo and in areas where the layer of *rofe* is relatively thin or in artificial dry-farmed beds.

Sheltering wall (*soco*) made with volcanic rock

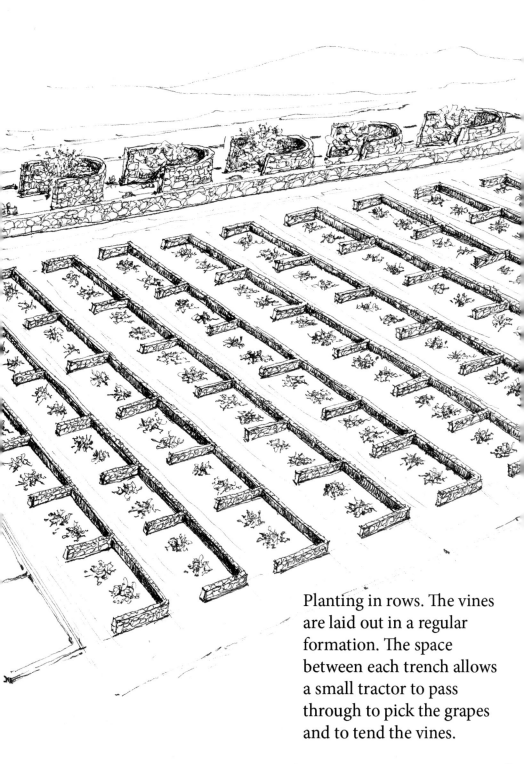

Planting in rows. The vines are laid out in a regular formation. The space between each trench allows a small tractor to pass through to pick the grapes and to tend the vines.

They also tend to be located in more modern farms which have a higher grape yield thanks to a higher density of planting.

3. Cultivation in lava fissures

This method of cultivation is used for grapevines or fruit trees, especially for varieties that require more water such as the Muscat grapes. It consists of planting at the bottom of hollows or cavities that have formed naturally in the volcanic lava flow where there is fertile soil. In this way the lava acts as a kind of funnel that directs any water collected straight into the plants. These fissures, or *chabocos*, as they are known locally, can be naturally formed where bubbles have burst in the lava flow or cracks have opened up in the lava. They can also be man-made either by digging away at the rock or by using dynamite.

The nature of these fissures means that they are generally difficult to access but you can see an example in the farm belonging to the El Grifo winery and in their Wine Museum.

4. Cultivation in vine arbours

This cultivation method, which is commonly used all over the globe consists of ensuring that new stems and grape clusters are raised off the ground. This is done by erecting a structure which is normally made of wood to a height of 1 to 3 metres. These arbours are usually built in terraces or in cracks in the petrified lava and are used mainly for Muscat grapes, as lifting them off the ground and keeping them well aerated helps guard against disease like *botrytis* or 'noble rot', to which they are particularly susceptible.

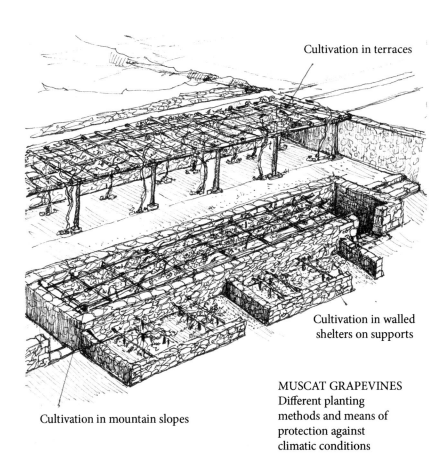

Cultivation in terraces

Cultivation in walled shelters on supports

Cultivation in mountain slopes

MUSCAT GRAPEVINES
Different planting methods and means of protection against climatic conditions

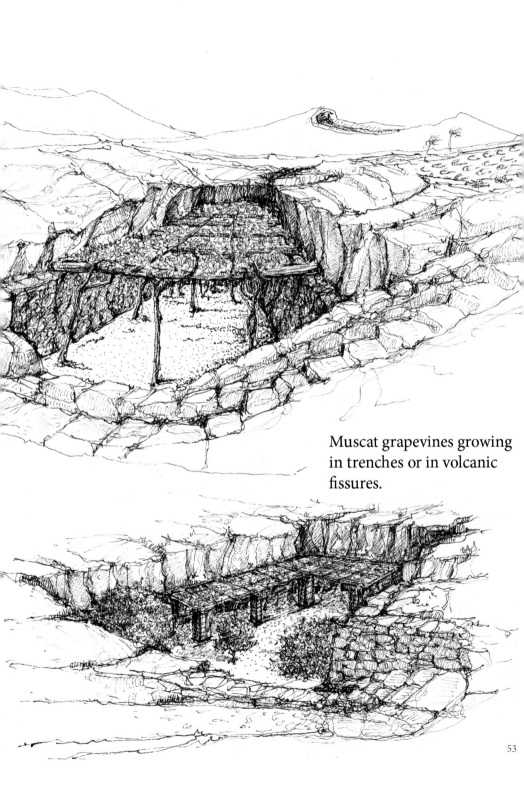

Muscat grapevines growing
in trenches or in volcanic
fissures.

53

5. Cultivation in terraces

Another method which is not as common but is in use in the north of the island is planting in terraces which make use of the mountain slopes.

The grape harvest

The grape harvest in Lanzarote is the earliest in Europe, starting in mid-July and continuing until early October. It is one of the most important tasks in the wine making process as it is the culmination of a year's work. Timing is key, as the viticulturists wait for the grapes to reach their optimum point of ripeness in order to obtain top quality wines. As the ideal moment to pick each grape variety differs, this tends to mean a long harvesting period. When the time is right, enormous care is taken to ensure the grapes reach the winery in the best possible conditions.

Harvesting marks an important point on the islanders' social calendar as there is an enormous number of small grape growers on the island, many of whom make their own artisan wines. Celebration of the Harvest Festival falls on the 15th August and coincides with the fiesta in honour of Our Lady of Charity (*La Caridad*). Festivities are held in the Bodegas La Geria winery and in other wineries near the chapel where they recreate typical traditional harvesting methods like using camels to transport the picked grapes and treading the grapes in an old wine press.

The grapes that reach the island's wineries either come from their own vineyards or their associated growers who receive a return of approximately 1.5 Euros per kilo. This sum is somewhat higher than in most other regions but is paid in a bid to compensate for the difficult growing conditions that mean such low production. With crop density of just 400 or 500 vines per hectare and an average yield of a mere 1,500 kilos per hectare, the cultivation system implemented in La Geria is unthinkable in any other part of the world. Climatic conditions present

another factor that impact on the harvest and subsequent wine production. Lack of rain (most vineyards do not have irrigation systems), heat waves, disease, and growth cycles can all seriously jeopardize the quality and quantity of the year's final yield.

A comparative study of wine production in Lanzarote between 1776 and the present day reveals how yields were considerably higher in the 18th century producing more than 3,000,000 kilos of grapes compared to the current average of 2,000,000 kilos. According to statistics produced by the Regulatory Board for the Designation of Origin (D.O) 'Lanzarote Wines', this is explained by the increase in the number of wineries registered to this Regulatory Board, which means that the same production of grapes is shared among a greater number of wineries.

Happily, wine consumption is on the rise and in 2010 a number of wineries were left with no surplus in their cellars at all, having sold more than 1,930,869 bottles of wine, well exceeding the average 1,630,000 bottles. Various initiatives such as putting into action the Island Council's Wine & Food Revitalization Plan, projects like *Saborea Lanzarote* ('Taste Lanzarote'), different marketing campaigns to promote the island's wines both on the island itself and overseas or the definitive approval of the La Geria Special Plan have all been contributing factors in helping to reverse the downward trend in consumption of Lanzarote D.O wines that had loomed large in 2009. In addition to these initiatives, the island's viticulturists and wineries themselves have been at pains to constantly improve the quality of Lanzarote wines. This is evident in the hundreds of awards obtained at regional, national and international events in recent years by different wineries under the auspices of the Regulatory Board. Lanzarote wines are better quality than ever and consumption is increasing, nevertheless, the landscape of La Geria is still in a precarious position as farms are being set aside and abandoned.

Harvesting Muscat grapes planted in arbours within a volcanic fissure. *Photograph by Leandro Viera, winner of the 3rd Photographic Competition run by Bodegas Los Bermejos winery.*

7. GRAPE VARIETIES

by Alberto González

There are many grape varieties on Lanzarote and although the Regulatory Board for the Designation of Origin (D.O) 'Lanzarote Wines' imposes no strong restriction on varieties used, those that predominate are the Malvasía Volcánica (also known as the Lanzarote Malvasía), white Listán Blanca, or Palomino grape, the red Listán Negra, the Muscat de Alejandría, and the Diego which is also known as 'Vijariego'. There are also other varieties like the Burra-blanca, Tinta Conejera, Breval and recently other new grapes have appeared from overseas such as the Merlot, Syrah, Tintilla, Baboso Negro, Cavernet Sauvignon and Negramoll.

The star variety on Lanzarote is without doubt the Malvasía Volcánica which has been recognized by the International Organisation of Vine and Wine (O.I.V.) as a variety in its own right. Only one genome has been identified in the world and it is believed that its various clones exist in Lanzarote. Isolation and negligible crossing with other types of grape make this variety the oldest Malvasía in the world. It originates from Asia Minor and Greece, and reference has been made to it for over 2,000 years. It arrived on Lanzarote en route from the Mediterranean to the islands of Tenerife and La Palma but did not reach Lanzarote until the 19th century. There are two varieties of Malvasía in the Canaries; Malvasía Volcánica and Malvasía Aromática, (or Malvasía La Palma). The latter being present in La Palma and in some areas of Tenerife.

Geographically-speaking different varieties can be found in most parts of the island but vineyards in certain areas lean towards growing specific varieties. Tinajo, for example, tends to grow the Malvasía Volcánica variety and to a lesser extent the Listán Negra and Muscat. Conil and Masdache, on the other hand, are home to vineyards that produce nearly all of the island's Diego grapes, especially the area of Masdache known as Juan Bello. However, Malvasía Volcánica and Palomino (Listán Blanca) are also grown in this area. In La Geria the majority of vineyards cultivate Palomino grapes (Listán Blanca), although Malvasía Volcánica and Listán Negra are also present on a smaller scale. In the Ye-Lajares region you will find mostly Listán Negra and then in equal parts Diego, and Malvasía Volcánica and Muscat.

In terms of identifying the ideal locations for growing specific varieties, it generally depends on their individual production capabilities and level of adaptability. The Diego grape fares well in the Juan Bello region of Masdache, perhaps because it benefits from the influence of the constant marine currents. The Malvasía Volcánica grape thrives in Tinajo because the soil is more fertile and there is more moisture. The Listán Negra has adapted especially well to conditions here and also in Ye-Lajares, meanwhile, Muscat grapes have adapted to the whole island.

Malvasía Volcánica

There are different clones of the Malvasía Volcánica variety, so some characteristics may vary slightly. The grape itself can be round or oval, depending on the clone, with speckled skin on clusters that are exposed to more direct sunlight. It is these sun-soaked clusters that are the most distinctive and have the best flavour. A typical cluster could weigh anything between half a kilo and two kilos. It is an aromatic variety with touches of Muscat flavour and perfume. It ripens early and is harvested towards the beginning of August. It is a vigorous vine with pale green, open leaves that turn a yellowish colour, depending on the stage in the growth cycle. The plant has adapted to the island's conditions and is resistant to its dry climate, wind and, above all, to the constant sun. However, it is very prone to diseases such as powdery mildew. Malvasía grapes are grown throughout the island, but especially in Tinajo.

Wine produced with Malvasía Volcánica grapes is balanced, high in acidity with tropical fruit aromas and notes of citrus and aromatic herbs.

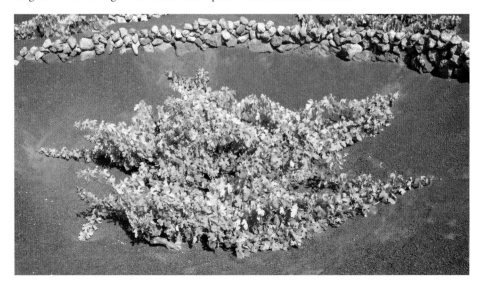

Palomino (Listán Blanca) & Listán Negra

It is a low vigour vine with light green foliage and palmate leaves. Even though it is highly resistant to diseases such as powdery mildew and mildew, the black variety is prone to infestation by cochineal.

The Listán grapes do not benefit from too many hours exposed to the sun which can cause them to lose their freshness and acidity, and in cases of extreme heat the black variety can even lose its colour. The grape and cluster are average-sized and both white and red grapes share similar characteristics. They are harvested in mid-August. The

wines from the Listán grapes are quite high in alcohol content and not fresh flavoured or particularly aromatic, especially the whites. The reds are more aromatic with notes of red fruits like mulberries and dried figs. They are light and medium-bodied wines which are not suitable for ageing.

Both the Palomino and Listán Negra varieties can be found all over Lanzarote, but especially in La Geria where the white Palomino variety predominates. In the north, however, in the Ye-Lajares region, it is the reds that prevail.

Muscat of Alexandria

The variety of Muscat grape found on Lanzarote is the Muscat of Alexandria which produces large oval grapes that are highly aromatic with delicate Muscat notes. The grapes grow in elongated clusters which can be loose or more compact depending on the year; this latter type tends to be better quality. It is a late harvesting grape that does not ripen until the beginning of September.

The leaves are large and serrated and dark green in colour. It is a high vigour plant, especially in wet years and it is very productive. The vine shoots are reddish in tone especially as they are forming. The vines are usually planted individually in volcanic fissures or in a low arbour as they need plenty of moisture. They are, however, highly prone to 'noble rot' or *botrytis*.

Muscat of Alexandria grapes produce sweet wines made with grapes that have undergone extended ripening. Their sweetness is evocative of a patisserie with notes of flowers and dried fruit.

In Lanzarote they are found in practically all areas of the island.

Diego

The Diego variety of grape is probably the least common on Lanzarote and in danger of disappearing altogether as cultivation has diminished over the last few years. They are almost exclusively grown in Masdache in the area known as 'Juan Bello'.

The leaves are deep green and with reddish coloured vine shoots that distinguish them from other varieties. The clusters are large and hold large grapes which can measure up to 4 cm in diameter. The plant is very resistant to disease and low-medium in vigour. They are late harvesting, the latest on the island, in fact, and are not picked until the end of September or early October.

It is not an aromatic grape but it lends wines great complexity as it is the most acidic of all the varieties on Lanzarote, and is ideal for ageing. Single varietal wines made only with Diego grapes are pleasant with hints of apple but the best results are achieved when it is blended with other varieties.

8. SOCIAL AND CULTURAL VALUES

Water and society

Up until a few decades ago the history of Lanzarote could be summarized as the saga of the never-ending battle against water scarcity. Essayist and poet Agustín Espinosa defined Lanzarote as 'a lopped off piece of Africa'. Indeed, it is an island where the serious lack of water supply has forced the population to devise a multitude of strategies to try and ensure their survival.

Water is the singular most important factor to have influenced how Lanzarote has evolved. There are many testimonials that bear witness to the shortage of water and its dramatic consequences such as emigration, poverty and social crisis. In the 19th century French traveller René Vernau was astonished at what he saw;

"When it rains it is amazing to see the lengths to which they go to collect the water!" He added, *"It is only when you are born in a country such as this that you can truly appreciate the value of water."* Canarian historian José Viera y Clavijo was even clearer; *"They do not speak of gold or silver, nor of jewels or other conventional belongings or passing fancies or desirable possessions, but rather of timely rains, of sowing seeds and of plentiful pastures."*

Many facets of the island's culture, traditions and technology are inextricably linked to finding a means to capture and store Lanzarote's scarce annual rainfall. They devised open reservoirs, water deposits, water galleries and wells which proved extremely effective on a small scale, yet so hard and demanding on those who built them. Nearly every aspect of life was affected in some way by the lack of water: the economy, local politics, the relationship with the landscape, architecture and power structures, including the domestic reality of each family. In agriculture, for example, they had to come up with ingenious and laborious solutions like making use of volcanic ash. In the field of civil engineering, the shortage of water brought about the creation of a large number of water catchment and storage systems. In the twentieth century, continued lack of water lead to new efforts in the search for a means of providing islanders with a safe and reliable water supply. This meant that large water reservoirs were built in the mid-1900s and underground water galleries were opened in the cliffs of Famara.

The island began to see an about-turn in its fortunes in 1965 when the Díaz Rijo brothers installed Europe's first water-treatment plant for urban use. Despite its initial teething problems, the waterworks were pivotal to bringing about the change that lead to the great developments that would take place in Lanzarote over the following decades.

Illustration by Santiago Alemán.

Chronicle of thirst

Even as recently as the 1960s, dramatic accounts described the anguish suffered by the lack of water. This piece was written by native of Lanzarote, Guillermo Topham, and published in weekly magazine *Antena*:

"[...] the drought in Lanzarote is unusual, different and unique; it is an inhuman, heart-wrenching dryness that means that it is sometimes impossible to quench your thirst.

For years, the lack of rainfall has condemned the people of Lanzarote to endless hours of dramatic want and bitterness. Children would beg, not for money, but for a bottle of water as they huddled together by the water trucks. Country women would prepare their stews using water previously used by neighbours. Housewives from the country would walk for miles from their village homes to distant beaches, as far as seven kilometres away, just to be able to wash their modest clothing. Weather beaten men, both young and elderly would traipse for miles across the island, with their small casks carried by donkeys and camels, just to stock up on water for their most basic of human needs. Crops and animals lay twisted by a cruel death due to the anguish of thirst."

Farmers, heroes of La Geria and Lanzarote

One of the clearest examples of how the shortage of water has shaped life in Lanzarote is in its traditional agriculture, and there can be no clearer example than that of La Geria. This landscape has combined productivity and aesthetics with respect for centuries-old customs. Motivated by the social status enjoyed by having their own wine at home with which to entertain guests and receive praise for the quality of their wine, viticulturists have carried out years of maintenance work in a delicate landscape and have consistently updated their wine making methods.

In order to prepare the land, the farmer would traditionally put a generous layer of *picón* granules on top of the fertile soil which is where the vine would be planted. This layer would sometimes be several metres thick and if it was in an area where it had accumulated naturally, a pit would be dug ready to place the vine at its centre. It is was as if the farmer would have to scratch around in the enormous black blanket of inert volcanic ash, looking for a safe spot, shielded from the prevailing winds by some rocks on the edge of the hollow. This work, often described as more akin to gardening, has been carried out for three centuries by hand and with the help of camels. The slightest movement around the pit means the *rofe* could easily fall, so farmers have to constantly dig it back out when the wall is being built. The whole process was a painstaking task for the impoverished farm labourers who for the most part did not own the lands they were working, but had no alternative other than to toil for long days in the hope that, with a little luck, the land would survive the constant dry spells. But for many it was not a matter of choice; either they worked from sunrise to sunset to try to minimize the lack of water or they had to turn their thoughts to the possibility of emigrating.

Wine making in Lanzarote has a valuable social component and a large proportion of the grape yield today is destined for artisan wine making. According to the Regulatory Board, there are more than 1,700 people currently working in the field of viticulture, either as professionals or as keen amateurs. Although the economic reward is limited, grape farming is of immense value in terms of the land and maintaining the landscape. Making artisan wines accounts for nearly 30% of total wine production and has formed a part of family life in Lanzarote for centuries. Every winery was, and still remains, a place for people to get together in social gatherings to chat, play cards share food and taste wines.

A group of viticulturists taking a break in La Geria and enjoying local produce such as cheese, sponge cake, dried salted whitebait and wine.

The work it takes to maintain the vineyards is often carried out by groups of family and friends on private lands and in the traditional wineries. The different jobs differ according to the seasons:

Winter
The pruning season begins in January, although it is most usual to do it with the waning moon in February. This process prepnares the vine to shed its leaves. If this is not carried out the vine will produce grapes that year but not in following years. At the same time as pruning, old leaves are collected and then buried under a layer of *rofe* to act as a kind of fertilizer. In March, as the first buds appear, sulphur is spread to prevent disease.

Spring
The grapevines are tended again in April and any non-productive branches, with few or no buds are removed. In May, more trimming is done to help air circulate and ensure the vines are well oxygenated. They are also checked and trimmed to prevent them from moving about in the wind and potentially destroying the pits.

Summer
In June the wineries get ready to receive the grapes that will be collected in the months of August until September. The traditional wineries, of which there are many on Lanzarote, clean their oak and chestnut barrels, or more recently steel casks, in preparation for the must. The grapevines can only be reached by following the paths in the gravel and accessing the pit on foot. This means that the harvest, and indeed all the work carried out in the vineyard is a highly labour intensive and totally manual task. However, the grape harvest is not only a time for hard physical labour, but also time for a party with family and friends. Sometimes there are three generations of the same family working together at any one time; all lending a hand to work in the field for the harvest.

Autumn
After the harvest, work focuses on making the traditional white wines, sweet wines, red and rosés. This wine is normally ready for drinking in November although there is also a tradition for making *aguapata* - a low-alcohol wine (8%) which can be drunk after 15 days. Autumn is a time for maintenance work to be carried out in the vineyard such as re-digging the pits if necessary, repairing the stone walls or putting down compost.

César Manrique, 'Harvest' 1990
Collage/card 69x50cm
© Fundación César Manrique

César Manrique, 1990. A woman collecting fruit, including grapes in the La Geria region. Manrique found inspiration in the farm labourers of Lanzarote and this is a theme which is reflected in many of his works. Manrique celebrated the relationship between the farm workers and nature in the form of many different murals, illustrations, sculptures and architectural pieces.

Women

The role of women in Lanzarote's historically poor and isolated rural society has long been extremely hard. Discrimination kept women away from education (illiteracy levels among women have always been much higher than among men) and the role of women in society was quite limited, as was their public presence and influence. On many occasions they were subject to prejudices of the ilk so skilfully portrayed by Tenerife-born writer, Rafael Arozarena, in his novel *Mararía*. It tells the story of a beautiful woman in a farming village on Lanzarote who suffers a cruel fate, a victim of disillusionment in love and restrictive social mores. The film version of this famous novel won a Goya for its cinematography in 1999 and the actress who played the part of the young Mararía was Goya Toledo, herself a native of Lanzarote.

Not only were women responsible for all the jobs around the home and for bringing up their children, but they also had to help maintain the family financially. An example of this is in the women of La Graciosa who, among other tasks, were charged with selling fish in the villages in the north of Lanzarote. To do so, they would have to make the crossing and then traipse all the way up Famara cliff, all the while carrying heavy baskets laden with several kilos of fish on their heads.

Life in the countryside was no less harsh. In regions like La Geria, the role of women was also key for they would be responsible for many tasks including planting crops, grape harvesting and also keeping the farmlands maintained, looking after the home, cooking, bringing up the children and working for long days that extended beyond sunrise to sunset. The wineries, on the other hand, were traditionally a male domain.

LANDSCAPE AWARDS

In 2013 Spain nominated La Geria as its only entry for the European Landscape Award. It was a finalist and short-listed by the Council of Europe which acknowledges territories that have strived to create an exemplary landscape, where landscape is understood to mean the sustainable combination of nature and human intervention.

In the same year, La Geria also received the International CICOP prize in the Canarian Cultural Landscape category. It was awarded to La Geria as a prime example of a cultural landscape created by the efforts of people to work in harmony with nature on an island which boasts exceptional heritage resources.

Women picking corn on the cob in the area called 'El Peñón'. Photograph from the 1950s reproduced by kind permission of Antonio Lorenzo

Architecture and craftwork

Lanzarote's viticulture not only reveals a great deal about the island's history and society, but also basic elements of the island's culture, especially those linked to agriculture which was historically the basis of the island's economy. Handicrafts related to farming and wine growing are an essential part of the island's cultural heritage. Numerous elements of basket weaving, carpentry, domestic furniture making or stone work are linked to the island's rural life and many traditions originated in the home and formed part of daily family life. Knowledge about textile weaving and making farm tools was passed down from generation to generation. This education within each household was thanks to the rich legacy of oral literature and musical folklore which had developed in rural society as a means of passing on knowledge through ballads, songs and story-telling.

Traditional architecture is also closely linked with the island's agriculture where the houses and vernacular architecture are recognized for the beauty of their simplicity and functional quality. Their clear, simple spaces made them perfectly suited to the environment in which they stood. They were humble houses in design, and even more so in decoration which was totally in keeping with the modest lifestyle of the farmers who built them.

In La Geria, however, there remain a few outstanding examples of manor houses which were built in a much grander style to reflect the ownership of important farm lands and estates. Their larger, more sophisticated features included the use of wood which was a luxury item on such an arid island. Wood was also an essential element in wineries, especially for barrel-making. Bodegas Rubicón winery has fine examples of traditional architecture related to wine making which they managed to preserve when they restored the winery, conserving the old house, cellar and water deposit. The Bodegas El Grifo winery boasts a traditional old winepress that dates back to 1775. They have also preserved the property's outbuildings and have recreated a traditional barrel-making workshop.

The La Caridad chapel (left) and the Bodegas Rubicón winery (right) that stand together in La Geria.

A noteworthy part of La Geria's architectural heritage is the La Caridad chapel which predates the volcanic eruptions of 1730 that created the landscape as it now stands. It was built in 1706 at the request of former vicar, and benefice, Diego Laguna Ayala. At the time, proprietorship of La Geria was shared among a small number of important landowners and the region was renowned for its fertile lands.

When the eruptions began in 1730, the La Geria estate was composed of the chapel, and the house which now accommodates the Rubicón winery. The whole estate was severely affected by the volcanoes' outpourings and by May 1731 it was completely buried under volcanic ash. But by the time the eruptions had come to an end in 1734, they had managed to unearth these buildings again. With the change in agricultural methods and the rise of the wine trade, this chapel gained in importance as there was an increase in the number of workers and residents in the area.

Archaeology

La Geria also boasts a very interesting archaeological heritage, despite the sheer quantity of elements that were buried by the historical eruptions in the 18th century. Outstanding finds include the Taro de Testeina, the dwellings on Mount Diama and the rock carvings in Guardilama.

The Taro de Testeina is a round structure with a domed roof. It is likely to have been a house which dates back to the ancient inhabitants of the island and was then inhabited thereafter. It predates the eruptions and belonged to the village of Testeina which was completely buried by volcanic ash. It is a valuable archaeological treasure as it is one of the few sites on Lanzarote which preserves this type of ancient roofed housing. It is located in Testeina (Masdache) on an abandoned farm

Casa Museo del Campesino

Standing right at the geographical heart of Lanzarote is the Casa Museo del Campesino, the museum that pays tribute to Lanzarote's farm workers. It is surrounded by farmlands that show different cultivation methods and marks the entrance to La Geria, the island's most spectacular agricultural landscape.

In 1968, Lanzarote-born artist César Manrique created the enormous sculpture that towers over the entrance to the museum called the *Fecundidad*, or 'Fertility Sculpture'. It rises up out of rocks formed by the Tajaste crag and is built out of recycled water tanks taken from boats, painted white and sculpted into different shapes. It is an abstract piece which manages to be incredibly dynamic, despite its size and has become an iconic landmark on the island. Manrique was always a great champion of the island's agricultural and architectural traditions and beyond the sculpture stands the museum which shows different features of the Lanzarote's traditional architecture like its balconies, chimneys, hip roofs, doors and windows, furniture and the typical white-washed walls with green woodwork. The museum belongs to the network of Centres of Art, Culture and Tourism. After Manrique's untimely death, the museum was expanded under the creative direction of artist Ildefonso Aguilar and now includes a restaurant and dining area serving typical local dishes, as well as spaces dedicated to traditional craftwork and cultural activities.

A deep cave dwelling with domed roof dating back to the times of the original inhabitants. After the Hispanic conquest of the island this dwelling was probably used again in the village of Testeina and was buried after the eruptions of 1730 -1736.

that stands between two volcanic outflows with vines and fruit trees growing in volcanic fissures in the lava flow. You can see here how they have built sheltering walls for the vines using stones which would appear to have been taken from old houses. Another relevant find here are some stone walls which were built prior to the eruptions and which were partially covered by the lava flow. In further excavations, experts have also unearthed pieces of imported ceramic.

Close to the Taro de Testina, on the side of Mount Negra you can visit an ancient water well that has been recently restored by Lanzarote Island Council's Cultural Heritage Service. Water deposits such as this were structures built to collect and store water. They form an integral part of the island's architecture as the shortage of water gave rise to the development of highly sophisticated culture of water engineering projects.

"On 1st September 1730, the earth opened up in Timanfaya"
by Ignacio Valderas

So begins the chronicle of the longest series of volcanic eruptions in the Canaries in modern history. They were eruptions of a scale that caused the destruction of the islanders' livelihoods and brought about a famine which led to the emigration of vast numbers of islanders; although many opted to stay and stand up to nature. Their fertile lands had been buried under a blanket of inert volcanic ash in which nothing could be planted. They tried to dig and unearth their lands, but it was in vain. In some places the layer of volcanic ash measured as much as 4 metres deep but they discovered that if they persisted and dug right down they could reach the fertile soil and they could plant their crops. Whereas beforehand they could only grow cereals, now they could grow grapevines and other types of fruit trees which were strong and sturdy and produced especially sweet and flavoursome fruit.

With little more than wooden spades and strong arms, farmers started to dig pits; men, women, the elderly and children all worked together to uncover the rich soil that lay hidden under the blanket of volcanic granules. And so it was that they planted grapevines and tended them until they harvested their fruit and it was in this way that one of the most impressive wine growing landscapes on earth was created.

The fruit of their labours was so extraordinary that farmers actually transported the ash laden on camels, taking it from areas where it lay in abundance to areas where it had not reached, spreading it on farmlands and creating artificial dry farmed land. In the centre of their fields they would plant corn, potatoes, tomatoes and pumpkins and on the perimeters surrounding their lands they would create trenches for grapevines. They also made the most of cracks, or fissures that appeared when the rivers of lava cooled down and solidified, sometimes widening them with picks and hammers so as to open a breach wide enough to plant grapevines that could grow as tall as trees.

The immense effort and imagination of Lanzarote's farmers managed to turn desperation into good fortune; converting a barren landscape into one full of life. Today, La Geria is one of the most popular natural attractions on Lanzarote and is visited by crowds of onlookers who admire the beauty of its scenery. The care and dedication with which the vines are hand-tended until ripe for picking, make Lanzarote's grapes a unique oenological jewel, steeped in the essence of La Geria.

Only when you see elderly people go to their farms at dawn and return after sharing another day of healthy, life-enhancing retirement with their vines; only when the time for harvesting arrives and you see whole families helping out with friends and neighbours, ending the day with parties and barbecues; only when a glass of the best wine is shared in friendly rivalry and with enormous pride yours stands out against the rest; only then can you truly understand how far-reaching viticulture is on Lanzarote; only then can you realise it forms an integral part of our culture, inextricably linked to our lives.

Mist, or low cloud, which sometimes falls at night. It is an important source of moisture as it filters rapidly through the layer of porous volcanic gravel, or *rofe*.

9. FOOD & WINE

It is impossible to talk about the wines of Lanzarote without making mention of the island's delicious cuisine, which serves as yet another example of the unique way in which the islanders work in harmony with nature and demonsrates the affinity between culture and terrain.

Canarian food is original and distinctive but Canarian cuisine in general, and Lanzarote cooking in particular, have their roots in Spanish and Mediterranean traditions whilst retaining strong links with Latin America and, to a lesser extent, the nearby African continent. Like many elements of Canarian culture, its cuisine has been shaped by its strategic geographical position and its connection with three continents which has had such a great influence throughout the history of the Canaries. However, it is Lanzarote that truly embodies what makes island fare so special; that is, the unique blend of water, land, wildlife and sea.

Lanzarote's agriculture has always been at the mercy of the island's shortage of water and this need has compelled islanders to devise ingenious but often arduous solutions to ensure their subsistence. One such solution was to plant crops in coarse dry sand (also called *jable* on the island) or use layers of volcanic ash. Their efforts have succeeded in cultivating superb quality produce such as cereals, pulses and vegetables for many centuries.

Lanzarote is especially noted for its potatoes and sweet potatoes which are typical in the Canaries. Despite the name, the *papa cría* is not actually a potato at all, but rather a prized fungi known as 'desert truffle' which grows naturally in sandy areas. Other products which are typically associated with Lanzarote are vegetables and pulses like onions, lentils and tomatoes which are all home grown, as well as chickpeas, peas, corn or chard. Fruit-wise the island grows watermelon, figs, melons, strawberries, papayas, blackberries and, of course, grapes.

Lanzarote enjoys a long fishing tradition in island waters and in the nearby African fishing grounds. Being one of the most important on the planet, it is replete with excellent specimens of tuna, snapper fish, stone bass, sea bream, moray, octopus, squid, sea bass or prawns, all of which are served fresh every day in the island's restaurants. A variety of shellfish: limpets, barnacles, sea snails and mussels are also readily available.

For meat-eaters, the island offers a range of choices; from small game like rabbits and fowl to other species like black pigs, that are native to the Canaries, and all varieties of goats which are kept for their meat as well as for making cheese; another important feature of Lanzarote cuisine. Traditionally, livestock farmers would use the leftover milk to make white cheese, soft cheese, semi cured and matured cured cheeses. Nowadays many cheesemakers have modernized traditional

75

Lanzarote Cocina

Lanzarote Cocina is a non-profit association comprised of a group of local restaurateurs and chefs who have teamed up to promote the island's home-grown produce and wines. It is dedicated to raising awareness about the advantages and unique appeal of local cuisine and the quality of the island's natural resources and produce.

The group of restaurants that come under the banner of *Lanzarote Cocina* have set out various objectives which outline this private undertaking's social responsibilities.

- to support and value primary sector produce on Lanzarote such as its lentils, vegetables, sweet potato, gofio, black pig, fish, cheeses etc.

- to promote and publicize the island's wines to ensure they are well represented on wine lists across the island.

- to cook dishes in accordance with stipulated quality control targets and promote the island's home-grown produce and local fish, whilst respecting the style and personality of the individual chef.

- to champion the preservation of Lanzarote's culinary and cultural heritage.

- to maintain an unwavering commitment to ensure Lanzarote remains faithful to a model of sustainable development.

methods and have received a number of awards for the quality of the cheeses presented at specialist food events.

Other elements that form an essential part of the island's typical cuisine include *gofio* which is a mixture of ground toasted cereals or spicy red and green *mojo* sauces which are an essential accompaniment to many dishes. Also typical to the Canaries is aloe vera with its numerous healing properties (the Canaries produce more aloe than any other region in Europe), and salt. The salt industry has had a significant role to play in Lanzarote's history. At the base of the Famara cliffs you can still see a fine example of natural salt works that have been used since ancient times. In the south of the island, the salt pans at Janubio are one of the biggest and most spectacular of their kind in the world. New companies have emerged in recent years and are breathing new life into the salt industry, exporting Lanzarote salt overseas with great success.

It would be an injustice to single out just a few delicious dishes as there are so many to choose from. However, it is worth naming certain typical dishes such as; starters like fish broth, lentil stew, corn soup, baked cheese with sauce or noodles with fish bass. Fish dishes include dogfish in onion sauce, marinated tuna, and octopus stew. Goat's meat is highly recommended as is pork belly. A delicious way of rounding off a meal is with desserts such as, milk and almond pudding, sweet potato turnovers (*truchas*) or honney fritters.

Lanzarote-style lentil stew.

Saborea Lanzarote ('Taste Lanzarote')

2010 saw the launch of *Saborea España* ('Tasting Spain'), a club created by Turespaña comprising different tourist destinations with gastronomic appeal.

All those involved, including restaurateurs, hotels, farmers, and wineries work together towards a common goal which is to offer tourists an authentic gastronomic experience; to raise people's awareness of the concept of gastro tourism whilst promoting local culture and cuisine; to improve and broaden the scope of what is currently on offer; to incorporate new ways of linking the primary sector to tourism; and to promote and market Spain's food and drink in a more ambitious and innovative way that will identify and capture new markets.

As a founder member, Lanzarote has formed an integral part of the project from its beginnings. Its *Saborea Lanzarote* ('Taste Lanzarote') initiative promotes the island's food and wines by creating innovative tourist experiences associated with its gastronomy and viticulture. *Saborea Lanzarote* is committed to attracting quality tourism by giving the island this added cultural and culinary dimension which sets it apart from typical sun, sea and sand destinations.

In December *Saborea Lanzarote* organizes its food and wine festival in Teguise which brings together the wine-making and food sectors in a celebration of local wares and gourmet delights. Visitors can watch presentations and take part in wine tasting and cookery workshops as well as sample a vast array of delicious dishes. In addition to organising this annual festival, every two months it holds themed food and wine weeks in different parts of the island designed to highlight different local produce. For more information you can consult their website at www.saborealanzarote.org.

Typical Lanzarote fish; parrot fish, gilthead sea bream, large-scaled scorpion fish, European barracuda and white sea bream.

Black pork

77

Perfect pairings of traditional cuisine and local wines

by Gustavo Palomo

Lanzarote wines provide the perfect accompaniment to the different dishes typical of Canarian cuisine. Sommelier Gustavo Palomo, winner of the best sommelier in the Canaries accolade in 2010 and again in 2012, suggests some perfect pairings of traditional Canarian cuisine and wines produced on the island. He has looked at each variety of grape typically grown on Lanzarote and devised a list of traditional dishes which make for a truly harmonious marriage of flavours. Most of these suggested pairings can be sampled in restaurants all over the island, whilst others are more adventurous and may surprise.

Malvasía Volcánica

- Perfect with all types of cheese: goat's cheese, sheep's cheese and cow's cheese. Especially the soft cheeses, semi-cured (cured for no longer than 3 months), Fuerteventura cheeses and *Guía* cheeses from Gran Canaria, etc.
- Wrinkly potatoes with red and green *mojo* sauces
- Boiled parrotfish
- Baked parrotfish
- Graciosa-style squid
- Salt fish with caramelized onions
- Conejero-style snapper fish
- Fish roe with seafood salad
- Sardines
- Fish broth
- Conger with rice
- Limpets and sea snails
- Whitebait
- Fish and seafood noodles

Diego

- Ideal with all types of cheese: goat's cheese, sheep's cheese and cow's cheese, especially soft cheeses, semi-cured (cured for no longer than 3 months), Fuerteventura cheeses and *Guía* cheeses from Gran Canaria, etc.
- Wrinkly potatoes with red and green *mojo* sauces
- Pan-fried limpets or limpet stew
- Olives with *mojo* sauces
- Catfish with *mojo* and coriander
- Squid stew
- Fried moray
- Baked snapper fish
- Baked parrotfish
- Fried comber fish
- Parrot fish rice
- Corn stew
- Vegetable stew
- Marinated rabbit

Sweet wines:
Malvasía Volcánica & Muscatel

- Especially good as an appetizer with aged goat's cheese and cheeses cured for more than 8 months.
- San Bartolomé's sweet potato turnover
- Meringues
- *Bienmesabe* (honey & ground almond dessert)
- Butter biscuits
- *Frangollo* (milk & almond pudding)
- Cheesecake
- Margucho-style honey fritters (La Graciosa)

Listán Negra (rosés)

- Suits pairing with all types of cheeses in the same way as Malvasía Volcánica and Diego
- Wrinkly potatoes with *mojo* sauces
- Olives with *mojo*
- Parrot fish rice
- Seafood rice
- Fish and seafood noodles
- Fish mousse
- Conejero-style chicken stew
- Stone bass croquettes
- Pea stew
- Baked vegetables

Listán Negra (reds)

- Perfect with all types of cheese: goat's cheese, sheep's cheese and cow's cheese cured for at least 4 months.
- Fried pork
- Catfish in sauce
- *Sancocho* (dried fish & sweet potato stew)
- Watercress soup
- Lanzarote-style lentil stew
- *Rancho canario* (meat stew)
- Kid goat - fried or stewed
- Marinated rabbit
- Meat stew
- Goat's meat stew
- Black-bellied pork
- Pork ribs with corn on the cob
- *Ropa vieja* (potato, chickpea & meat stew)

10. WINERIES GUIDE

The Regulatory Board for the Designation of Origin (D.O) 'Lanzarote Wines' came into effect on 14th December 1993; its objective being to guarantee the quality of the wines produced on Lanzarote and to certify their origin. To this end, exhaustive checks are carried out from the moment of harvesting right through to when the wine is actually bottled. Throughout the process the grapes and the wines undergo thorough testing, tasting and analysis. When a wine passes these tests it receives the Board's seal of approval in the form of a number which appears on the label, together with the logo, so that it can be easily recognized by consumers. This label acts as a guarantee that the wine has been made with grapes from the island and that it has passed all the stringent quality control checks.

There are 18 of the island's wineries working under the auspices of the Regulatory Board together with 1,700 grape growers. These wineries produce an average of 1,500,000 bottles; half of which are exported either overseas or to other Canary Islands and the other half stay on the island for domestic consumption. Approximately 15% of bottled wine is exported to the rest of Spain and other countries such as Germany, the United Kingdom and the United States. Lanzarote wines are not only noted for the extraordinary landscape of the wine growing region, but also for the excellent quality of the wines themselves which have received numerous international awards.

Many of the wineries that fall under the remit of the Regulatory Board are located in or around the region of La Geria. Given their privileged setting, some of the big wine producers have opened their doors to the public, offering different services associated with selling wines such as tastings, guided visits, museums, restaurants or shops. They are also often used as venues for special tastings and other cultural or open-air events. These wineries are; El Grifo, Vega de Yuco, Los Bermejos, La Geria and Rubicón.

There are other wineries belonging to the Regulatory Board which can be visited by prior appointment: Bodegas Castillo de Guanapay, Guigan, La Florida, El Alto, El Campesino, La Grieta, Martinón, Mozaga, Reymar, Viña Meseta and Vulcano de Lanzarote.

Lanzarote wines can be purchased in supermarkets, restaurants or in the airport. To buy certain wines from small producers it is best to contact the winery directly which will provide information about the different points of sale.

LANZAROTE WINERIES

Bodegas Castillo de Guanapay

Tel. (34) 928 804 579
La Asomada, nº 39, Tías

Bodegas El Alto

Tel. (34) 928 173 510
Las Quemadas, nº 12, La Vegueta, Tinajo

Bodegas El Campesino

Tel. (34) 678 753 133
Guadarfía, nº 2, San Bartolomé

Bodegas El Grifo

Tel. (34) 928 524 036
LZ-30, km. 11, San Bartolomé
www.elgrifo.com

Bodegas Guiguan

Tel. (34) 928 840 715
Avenida de los Volcanes, nº 116, Tinajo
www. bodegasguiguan.com

Bodegas La Geria

Tel. (34) 928 173 178
La Geria main road, km. 19
www.lageria.com

Bodegas La Grieta

Tel. (34) 928 848 110
Cueva de los Verdes, nº 5,
Punta Mujeres, Haría

Bodegas La Florida

Tel. (34) 928 593001
La Florida 89
San Bartolomé
www.bodegalaflorida.com

Bodegas Los Bermejos

Tel. (34) 928 522 463
Camino a los Bermejos, nº 7, La Florida
San Bartolomé
www.losbermejos.com

Bodegas Martinón

Tel. (34) 928 834 160
Camino del Mentidero, nº 2, Masdache,
Tías
www.bodegasmartinon.com

Bodegas Mozaga

Tel. (34) 928 520 485
Arrecife-Tinajo main road, km. 8, Mozaga,
San Bartolomé

Bodegas Reymar

Tel. (34) 928 840 737
Plaza de Los Dolores, nº 19, Tinajo
www.bodegasreymar.com

Bodegas Rubicón

Tel. (34) 928 173 708
Teguise-Yaiza main road, nº 2
www.vinosrubicon.com

Bodegas La Florida

Tel. (34) 928 593 001
La Florida, n 89
www.bodegaslaflorida.com

Bodegas Tierra de Volcanes

Tel. (34) 630 889 454
Las Vistas, nº 18, Yaiza

Wineries

1. Castillo de Guanapay
2. El Alto
3. El Campesino
4. El Grifo
5. Guiguan
6. La Geria
7. La Grieta
8. Los Bermejos
9. Martinón
10. Mozaga
11. Reymar
12. Rubicón
13. Stratvs
14. Tierra de Volcanes
15. Vega de Yuco
16. Viña la Meseta
17. Vulcano de Lanzarote
18. Bodegas La Florida

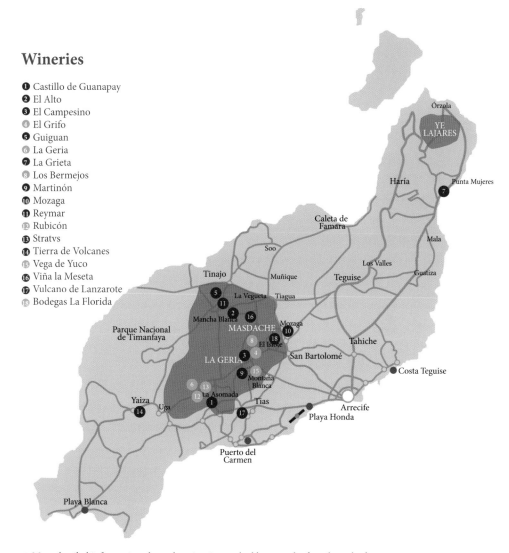

● More detailed information about the wineries marked here can be found overleaf.

Bodegas Vega de Yuco

Tel. (34) 928 524 316
Camino del Cabezo, s/n, Masdache, Tías
www.vegadeyuco.es

Bodegas Viña Meseta

Tel. (34) 928 840 425
Camino El Peñón, nº 14, La Vegueta,
Tinajo

Bodegas Vulcano de Lanzarote

Tel. (34) 928 524 469
C/ Víctor Fernández Gopar, nº 5, Tías
www.bodegavulcano.es

Bodegas El Grifo

Founded in 1775, it is the oldest winery in the Canaries and ranks among the ten oldest in Spain. It boasts production of more than 500,000 litres per year although it has capacity for 1.2 million litres. It has its own vineyard which measures some 60 hectares and carries out consultancy work with its associate viticulturists. Its sustainable integrated production system of farming has been certified and it was the first winery in the Canaries to introduce modern technology such as automated bottling, stainless steel fermentation tanks and cooling systems. It has taken part in a research and development project in collaboration with the University of Montpelier.

The distinctive palm tree that stands proudly in the estate dates back to 1750 and is probably one of the oldest on the island and the Muscat grape arbours that can be seen on guided visits date back to the 19th century. The winery still conserves wines produced in 1881 and is careful to maintain traditional techniques in the production of its aged Malvasía Canari and George Glas wines.

El Grifo offers visitors the chance to explore the history of wine production on Lanzarote by wandering around the Wine Museum housed in the old winery with displays of different utensils used by wine makers in the 19th and 20th centuries and a walk through part of the vineyard itself. All of their wines can be tasted in the specialist shop.

The winery also boasts a library of at least 5,000 books about wine which was opened in 1998. César Manrique was a family friend and it was he that came up with the distinctive griffin logo for the winery and one of its wines. He was also responsible for encouraging them to create the present-day museum that stands in the ancient winery. El Grifo often hosts cultural evenings and takes an active part in many cultural events in the region.

Wines

The winery has 16 different wines including (from left to right) the Dry collection, Semi-sweet collection, Listán Negro red, Ariana red, and the sweet Malvasía Dulce and Malvasía Canari.

WEBSITE: www. elgrifo.com
ADDRESS: LZ-30 main road at 11 kms
San Bartolomé, 35550
TELEPHONE: (34) 928 524 036
FACILITIES: guided tours, wine museum, tastings, cultural events and specialist shop

Other wines produced are the rosé fermented in oak casks, the sweet Muscatel de Ana, Natural sparkling wine, dry white and rosé. Listán Negro sweet red, organic dry Malvasía, and a Syrah reserve red.

Wine Museum

The museum was opened in 1982 and is one of the most popular of its kind in Spain, welcoming more than 60,000 visitors per year. It is housed in the old winery built in 1775. Visitors are treated to a brief history of wine making on Lanzarote and can see old machinery used at the end of the 19th century and the start of the 20th century. You can also visit the workshop where the barrel-makers would make the casks, the library, which houses more than 5,000 volumes about wine, as well as the old fermentation tanks where wine was once made in this winery. A visit also includes a tour of the vineyards where you can see Muscat grapevines that have survived for hundreds of years planted in volcanic fissures as well as fruit trees and vineyards of Malvasía Volcánica grapes.

OPENING HOURS: Monday to Sunday (including public holidays) 10.30 am - 6 pm Guided tours at 11 am, 1 pm, 4 pm and 5 pm. Telephone: (34) 928 524 951

Bodegas La Geria

The La Geria winery stands next to the La Caridad chapel on top of a hill and enjoys spectacular views of the surrounding countryside and Timanfaya National Park. It was built towards the end of the 19th century by the Rijo family and was acquired by its current owners and directors in 1993. Its annual production is approximately 250,000 litres. Apart from the winery buildings, there is a restaurant, a tasting room, a shop selling handicrafts and a large car park. La Geria winery receives some 400,000 visitors per year which makes it the most visited winery on Lanzarote and among the most popular places to visit on the whole island, as well as one of the most visited wineries in Spain.

The La Geria winery is often the only point of contact that many visitors have with the island's wine sector as it has long been on the tourist route. Its superb views across to Timanfaya make it one of the most popular vantage points for taking stunning photographs of the island.

The winery's tasting room is well worth a visit with its ancient pressing vat, the traditional wine press and its floor covered with *rofe* which is typical of all the artisan wineries.

Wines

The winery boasts 9 different types of wines; the dry Malvasía Volcánica, the sweet Dulce, the dry Manto made with Malvasía Volcánica, the Muscatel and red Tinto Selección, the semi-sweet Malvasía Volcánica, the carbonic macerated red, Tinto and its Tinto.

WEBSITE: www.lageria.com
ADDRESS: Carretera La Geria main road at 19 kms
TELEPHONE: (34) 928 173 178
FACILITIES: specialist shop, restaurant, handicrafts shop and guided tours.

Harvest Festival

A harvesting and grape crushing party is held by the La Geria winery on 15th August every year to coincide with the festivities in honour of *La Caridad* (Our Lady of Charity). On this day harvesting is carried out by hand, by men and women dressed in typical clothes and camels are used to carry the precious cargo. The grape stomping is done in the old wine press using the ancient method of treading the grape barefoot. Locals and tourists are invited to take part. This festival offers a superb glimpse into grape growing in the past and serves as a reminder as to just how arduous a task it was, and remains today. Taking part in this event is one of the best possible ways to get to know the landscape and the culture of La Geria. This day is also celebrated with activities in other wineries in the region.

Bodegas Los Bermejos

The Los Bermejos winery was founded in 2001 and takes its name from the estate in which it stands in the Juan Bello region of the San Bartolomé municipality. Although the winery was only established relatively recently, it is part of an 18th century manor house which once belonged to one of the island's most influential families in an area with a long tradition of grape growing. The old manor house has been restored along with other winery outbuildings and the ancient wine press. The winery currently produces an average of 400,000 litres every year.

Today, Los Bermejos has made an excellent name for itself as a producer of high quality wines. They use processes and machinery designed to preserve and maintain all the natural flavours. A great deal of effort is put into growing the best possible grape and therefore the best wine.

"Lanzarote has given us the great gift of conditions unrivalled anywhere else in the world: climate, soil, grape varieties, unique cultivation methods - this land has provided everything. All that remains for us to do is bottle the fermented juice of these grapes, without the need for manipulating them, transforming them or trying to improve them in any way."

The bottle they use is very distinctive in shape and it is one of the wines most readily found outside the island. Together with El Grifo, it produces the most wine and boasts the most associate viticulturists. The winery was opened to the public recently and now offers guided visits and a specialist shop.

Los Bermejos is committed to making organic wines like their Diego, their dry Malvasía and their rosé. They also implement sustainable procedures like using FFC certified corks.

Wines

Los Bermejos winery has 14 different wines on the market including; (from left to right) dry Malvasía and rosé Malvasía, its carbonic maceration red, Tinto, the naturally sweet Malvasía and its dry sparkling Brut Nature. Other wines are the red Tinto, naturally sweet Moscatel, the brut dry rosé and organic Diego.

WEBSITE: www.losbermejos.com
ADDRESS: La Florida, San Bartolomé, Camino a los Bermejos, 7
TELEPHONE: (34) 928 522 463
FACILITIES: specialist shop, guided tours, food and cultural events.

The Los Bermejos Photography Competition

Among the numerous events run by the Los Bermejos winery is its photography competition which encourages entrants to capture the unique nature of wine growing in Lanzarote. The competition started in 2010 and focussed on subjects like the landscape, the harvest and the actual wineries themselves. The competition attracts a huge number of participants from all over the world. The last few competitions have had an added social dimension as it is not only the winning photographers who are awarded prizes, but the viticulturists also receive an award in acknowledgement of the important role they have to play in maintaining the landscape. The winery organises an annual exhibition to display the entries. You can consult their website for rules and information on how to participate on www.losbermejos.com and see winning entries from previous year's competitions.

Photograph by Christian Piesch, winner of the 2nd edition of the photographic competition.

Bodegas Rubicón

This winery is located in the heart of La Geria in 18th century house and winery opposite the La Caridad chapel and the La Geria winery. The current owners acquired it from the Fajardo family in 1979 and undertook considerable restoration work, taking care to preserve many of the original features of the old house and converting it into the winery as it stands today.

The house and the La Caridad chapel belong to the group of buildings originally called the 'La Geria Estate' which was built by Don Diego Laguna at the turn of the 18th century. The way the house and subsequently the winery have changed with the times mirrors how wine making has evolved in Lanzarote; what had been a simple artisan winery is now one of the most popular spots for tourists to visit in La Geria. The winery is made up of a cellar, restaurant, exhibition hall, tasting room, barrel room, conference room, shop and ancient wine press. The old wine press is made of excavated stone and sunk into the ground. There are also displays of traditional utensils like a 20th century press and cement tanks that were used to store the wine.

Bodegas Rubicón opened its doors to visitors in 2009. Apart from inviting visitors to explore the winery, it also hosts regular wine tasting events and works with promoters to hold a variety of events in its facilities.

On average, the Rubicón winery produces around 150,000 litres of wine per year, although it has a maximum capacity of 300,000 litres. In 2012, it won, among other accolades, the Gold Medal award in the 17th Berliner Wein Trophy awards in Berlin and the Golden Bacchus award in the 10th International Bacchus Wine Competition held in Madrid.

Wines

The winery has 9 varieties of wine in its cellars; the Amalia, a dry white Malvasía, Rubicón dry, Rubicón Muscatel, the Sweet Gold (Muscatel) and the duo of Don Diego and Doña Dulce wines made with Diego and Muscat grapes.

WEBSITE: www.vinosrubicon.com
ADDRESS: La Geria main road, at 19 kms
TELEPHONE: (34) 928 173 708
FACILITIES: specialist shop, exhibition hall, restaurant and guided tours.

Restoration of the House

Building of La Geria estate began as far back as the 16th century with written papers to that effect dated 1570. The La Caridad chapel belonged to the estate and was built by vicar and benefice Don Diego Laguna Ayala in 1706. The eruptions which lasted from 1730 to 1736 left the chapel and parts of the estate buried under a blanket of volcanic ash. In 1734, the chapel was cleared from under its volcanic rubble and restored as a place of worship before the eruptions came to a halt. The latest restoration work was undertaken by the current owners in 2009 and respects the layout of the original estate. Visitors can see the results of the excavation work and enter inside the old water storage deposit which has been converted into a wine tasting room.

Bodegas La Florida

This is the latest winery to join the Regulatory Board for the Designation of Origin (D.O.) 'Lanzarote Wines' (2014). It stands right in the geographical heart of the island in the village of La Florida in an old 19th century manor house. It boasts more than 200,000 m² of land, a wide volcanic lava cavern and an ancient Canarian dragon tree that is said to be more than 270 years old. As you approach the vineyard, visitors are greeted by the sight of this dragon tree which has become the winery's iconic logo and has propagated many other dragon trees on Lanzarote.

The winery is also home to other treasures like the stunning volcanic bubble in the lava flow which is more than 160 metres wide where an impressive eucalyptus tree looms large. You can also wander around the volcanic fissures and see how the Muscat grapes are grown.

The enormous manor house is a listed building and once belonged to Luis Ramírez (1884 - 1950) one of the island's great culture and education benefactors. Ramirez donated his property and land to the Salesian monks, including his personal library, on condition that any profit they made would be set aside to finance education grants for young people in Lanzarote.

The current owner, Ginés González Viera, has restored the buildings, conserving traditional features like the wine press, the threshing floor and the water deposit. The winery produced its first wines in 2012 and has been a member of the Regulatory Board for the Designation of Origin (D.O.) 'Lanzarote Wines' since 2014. Its wines are created using mostly Malvasía Volcánica grapes and produces on average 30,000 litres every year from its own vineyards which produce different varieties of grapes including Malvasía Volcánica, Muscat, Palomino, red Listán Negra, Syrah (Shiraz) and Tempranillo grapes.

Wines

The winery makes 5 different types of wines and is especially noted for its dry Malvasía, the red, the muscatel, rosé and semi-dry.

WEBSITE: www.bodegaslaflorida.com
ADDRESS: 89, Calle La Florida
TELEPHONE: (34) 928 593 001
FACILITIES: gourmet shop, visits, private event hire etc.

Gourmet shop and Events

Bodegas La Florida has embraced the beauty of its natural surroundings and impressive buildings and created a place which will truly delight visitors. The lava bubble, the gardens and the three different rooms all offer stunning venues for all types of occasions, especially weddings and corporate events.

A gourmet shop has also been opened offering a selection of the bodega's own wines and delicatessen treats. Opening hours are Monday to Saturday 11 am till 4 pm.

Bodegas Vega de Yuco

The Vega de Yuco winery was founded in 1997 and is located on a family-run estate in Masdache. It produces an average of 150,000 litres per year and aims to produce a quality wine which is the result of combining traditional methods with modern technology. It has a specialist shop and offers guided visits to its vineyards including its impressive botanical garden which boasts more than 60 different plant species that are native to the island. This beautifully kept garden gives fascinating information about the different species that grow all over the island and are gathered together here in one remarkable space.

Vega de Yuco is also dedicated to producing sweet liqueurs and in so doing has revived the social and cultural traditions that have long surrounded liqueur making on the island. For many centuries liqueurs have been an essential part of many local fiestas or social gatherings. The winery has recently published a book about Lanzarote's artisan liqueurs with information gathered by Giovani Lemes after speaking to many artisans on the island. More information about the book can be found on the winery's website www.vegadeyuco.es.

The winery holds the ISO 14001 standard which certifies its ecological processes and respect for the environment as well as its efficient and responsible waste management programme and commitment to alternative energy.

For wine tasting and the shop, the winery is open to the public Monday to Friday from 10 am to 3 pm. Guided tours need to be booked in advance by phoning:
(34) 928 524 316.

Wines

The Vega de Yuco winery has a wide variety of wines and liqueurs on sale including; Dry white Malvasía, Yaiza dry Malvasía, its barrel fermented Yaiza Barrica, the delicately sparkling Vega de Yuco +dache and many liqueurs including its mulberry liqueur.

WEBSITE: www.vegadeyuco.es
ADDRESS: Masdache, Tías, Camino de Cabezo s/n 35572
TELEPHONE: (34) 928 524 316
FACILITIES: liqueurs, specialist shop, guided tours and garden of autochthonous plants.

Vega de Yuco's shop and tasting room is where visitors can sample its wines and liqueurs made following traditional recipes. There is also a terrace with stunning views over La Geria and a botanical garden with many varieties of local plants.

11. WHAT TO DO IN LA GERIA

The very nature of any landscape is that it is a complex and ever-changing territory and this is very much the case of La Geria. It is where agriculture, industry, commercial and tourist interests converge and where a vast number of people invest their hard work and fortunes; from individual viticulturists and wineries to public institutions and private companies who want to inject new vitality into the region. Whilst the area's unique cultivation method has generated an unrivalled spectacular landscape, the limited harvest and labour-intensive manual work involved take their toll. For this reason, there has been an impetus to promote alternative activities that complement the wine industry and open up the region to visitors who wish to actively explore the incredible scenery. The idea is 'to explore in order to appreciate and to appreciate in order to taste'. La Geria lends itself to such exploration as visitors can get involved and experience it firsthand or simply sit back and taste its delicious wines. This guide aims to compile the options available to visitors (apart from the wineries and activities already outlined) and highlight a whole host of activities which take place in La Geria and the surrounding areas, whether they are connected with the countryside, the wine or the island's cuisine.

Although the places and events listed here are long established, it is always a good idea to consult the organisations directly at the following addresses:

The Regulatory Board for the Designation of Origin 'Lanzarote Wines'

www.dolanzarote.com

Lanzarote Island Council (Cabildo de Lanzarote)

www.cabildodelanzarote.com

Saborea Lanzarote ('Tasting Lanzarote')

www.saborealanzarote.org

Events, sports & leisure

www.lanzarotewinerun.com
www.senderismolanzarote.com
www.sonidosliquidos.com
www.turismolanzarote.com
www.lanzarotedeportes.com
www.lanzarotenbici.com

Culture & tradition

www.artesaniadelanzarote.com
www.cactlanzarote.com
www.memoriadelanzarote.com
www.agrolanzarote.com
agustinpallares.blogspot.com.es

Museums and places to visit

Apart from the Wine Museum in the El Grifo winery (see page 85) and the Monumento al Campesino (see page 69), the guided tours around the wineries and other places of interest related to the island's wine-making culture are all highly recommended.

Tanit Museum

In the town of San Bartolomé, just a few kilometres away from La Geria, there is a museum dedicated to the island's farming and wine-making heritage. The Tanit Ethnographic Museum is housed in an 18th century Canarian manor house located in the heart of San Bartolomé, close to the town's church. It is a privately-run museum which exhibits a collection of belongings and tools used up until the mid 20th century and has displays relating to typical Canarian architecture and flora. Agriculture and viticulture are two fundamental themes running through the museum. The winery is fascinating and boasts an old wooden wine press that was in use from 1780 until 1902 and remains in good condition today. For more information contact: www.museotanit.com

El Patio Museum

This typical agricultural farm is in the village of Tiagua, very close to La Geria and the Casa-Monumento del Campesino (Monument to the Farm worker). The old farmhouse has been converted into an ethnographic museum dedicated to recreating and exhibiting many of the island's ancient traditions and ways of life. The museum buildings are fine examples of traditional architecture with original features like the old manor house itself, the wine press, the winery, the mill house and mill and the chapel. There is a wide variety of farm utensils and tools on display as well as traditional furniture that all bring to life the hardships and precarious nature of farm life on the island. The museum also has pleasant gardens and farmlands and offers wine tastings in its cellar. It has received the *Importantes del Turismo* award in recognition of the service it offers tourists. For further information, contact:
Telephone (34) 928 52 91 34

Tourist Centres

In the 1960s the Lanzarote Island Council came up with an innovative way to reverse the prevailing economic gloom on the island and embarked upon an ambitious, but ground-breaking project to build a network of Centres of Art, Culture and Tourism that would create artistic attractions out of stunning natural spaces. These centres are now credited with showcasing what makes Lanzarote such a remarkable island to visit and celebrate its history of volcanic eruptions and unique culture. By visiting the CACT you can appreciate what an enormous undertaking their creation was. In fact, it what was one of Spain's most ambitious cultural initiatives in the sixties. Local artist César Manrique was at the helm and he worked with a team of extraordinarily talented names. The Casa-Monumento del Campesino, or the Monument to the Farm Worker, is the Centre that is most closely related to the world of agriculture and is located just at the entrance to the La Geria region. Other marvellous Centres not to be missed are the Mirador del Río vantage point, the Jameos del Agua subterranean lava cavern and lake, the Cueva de Los Verdes caves, the Jardín de Cactus cactus garden, the MIAC contemporary art museum and, of course Timanfaya. For further information, contact: www.cactlanzarote.com.

Timanfaya & Visitors' Centre

A stroll around an area as awe-inspiring as Timanfaya is an experience visitors are unlikely to ever forget. The Fire Mountains stand in a vast expanse of land forever transformed by the volcanic eruptions that took place in the 18th century and they are, perhaps, one of Lanzarote's most iconic images. The visual impact of the volcanic cones, swathes of volcanic ash and petrified lava flows gives it an unearthly feel that both transports you to another planet whilst at the same time evoking the primeval beginnings of Earth. No visit to Timanfaya would be complete without stopping for refreshments at the impressive El Diablo restaurant, another of Manrique's works created in conjunction with his team of collaborators. It is also well worth visiting the Visitors' Centre in Mancha Blanca where you can learn all about volcanology in the Canaries and the series of eruptions that befell Lanzarote. To learn more about César Manrique you can visit the Foundation that bears his name located in his former home in Tahiche.

Activities

A Suggested Walk through La Geria Valley
by Ignacio Romero-Senderismo Lanzarote

WALK FACT SHEET

Departure: Between the Rubicón and La Geria wineries on the LZ-30 main road.
Arrival: Bodega Stratvs on the LZ-30 main road.
Distance: 2 kilometres
Approximate timing: 30 minutes

Since the volcanic eruptions spread their blanket of ash over most of the island, many hiking trails and paths have been worn into the 'volcano', as locals refer to the whole area of land covered by volcanic lava and debris. The island's ancestors created these paths in the newly formed terrain as they traipsed from their new homes to their farmlands. The unique landscape that we see today in La Geria was created little by little as a result of effort, sacrifice and survival. La Geria will stay alive as long as its vines and fruit trees live on, together with its gardeners, who perhaps unbeknown to them, are fighting for the preservation of their environment and landscape.

Walk description

This walk takes you through the centre of the valley and region of La Geria. The departure point is the old La Geria Estate and La Caridad chapel and the end is at the Barranco del Obispo ravine.

The walk starts in the heart of La Geria leaving from the Rubicón and La Geria wineries and the La Caridad chapel. This small white chapel miraculously survived the Timanfaya eruptions. Head for the LZ-30 main road heading north and just 50 metres along take the trail on the left heading west.

On either side of this path covered in volcanic ash (also known as *rofe* / lapilli / *picón*) you can see the deep pits that were painstakingly dug long ago in order to plant the vines and fruit trees into the fertile soil which can be found deep down under the thick layer of black ash.

As you approach Mount Diama the path splits, you need to take the right fork here,

although if your curiosity gets the better of you, you could keep going straight ahead a few metres and see the view of some of the lava flow and cones of the Fire Mountains. Not too far away there once stood some noble manor houses like Diama, Juan Gante, El Chupadero and Santa Catalina which were all buried by the volcanoes that erupted in the 18th century.

The path continues around the side of Mount Diama and leaves this ancient cone behind on the west. Keep heading northwards and check out the tree which is found all over La Geria, the fig tree. Figs were so abundant and such a common part of the islanders' diet that even today it is simply referred to as *fruta*, or 'fruit'. As you reach some houses you will come to a fork in the path; straight ahead continues in the same northwards direction that you have been taking until now, but you need to turn right and head eastwards. Look out for some ancient water wells in ruins which predate the eruptions that took place in the 18th century. Numerous wells of this kind were unearthed as farmers dug away at the layers of volcanic ash in order to plant their crops. Many have been restored and are functioning water deposits once more.

As you continue towards the LZ-30, turn northwards and you will arrive at the Bodegas Stratvs winery which stands at the end of the ravine called Barranco del Obispo and this marks the end of your walk.

Places of Interest

Ermita La Caridad Chapel
The chapel was built in the heart of the old La Geria Estate in honour of the Virgin La Caridad whose feast days falls on August 15th. This festival is linked to the grape harvest and marks the end of the arduous process of planting, pruning, cleaning, weeding, trimming, spraying sulphur and finally harvesting; from this point on the work of producing the wine passes into the hands of the wineries.

Cortijo La Geria
The grand La Geria Estate is located in the centre of the La Geria region. It belonged to Diego Laguna the vicar incumbent of Lanzarote and member of the Fajardo family. Today, it the Bodegas Rubicón winery.

Diama
This is the name of the mountain on the north side of the La Geria valley. It is said to be named after the manor house that completely disappeared under the lava flow that emanated from Timanfaya in the 18th century.

Juan Gante
This is the name of a small village that was once located near the village of El Chupadero but it was totally buried by the lava flow from the Timanfaya eruptions in the 18th century.

El Chupadero
The mountain located on the southwest side of La Geria valley takes the name El Chupadero after the village that once stood to its northwest before being buried under the mighty Timanfaya eruptions in the 18th century.

Santa Catalina
This was once an important village before it was engulfed by the Timanfaya eruptions in the 18th century.

Activities

La Geria

This is the name of the region that is home to countless numbers of vines planted in volcanic ash. Today the name also encompasses the entire area that comes under the auspices of the Protected Landscape of La Geria. It is also the ancient name of the small village of the same name that was buried by the volcanic lava flow spewed out by Timanfaya in the 18th century.

Crops

The grapevine is the most common crop grown in this region. The unique cultivation method used here has created a spectacular landscape which lends the region, and indeed the island, its distinctive identity. The sheer effort and manual work entailed in planting the vines and their subsequent care, which is more akin to the lovingly careful process of gardening, make the end product; the wines produced in the wineries all the more appreciated. The most commonly grown grape varieties are the Palomino, Malvasía and Diego.

Other fruit trees that are grown here include fig trees, mulberry bushes, guava trees, pear trees, lemon trees, oranges trees, carob trees, avocados and mango trees.

Flora

When you follow the suggested walk detailed overleaf you will see a number of species of flora. This includes:
Mediterranean saltwort (*Launaea arborescens*), Wavy heliotrope, or 'Camel's tongue (*Heliotropium ramosissimun*), Tree tobacco (*Nicotiana glauca*), White saladillo, or 'Bird's tongue' (*Polycarpaea nivea*), Rose geranium (*Pelargonium capitalum*), Lanzarote trefoil lotus (*Lotus lancerottensis*), Canary sorrel (*Rumex lunaria*), Spiny rush (*Juncus acutus*), Canary helianthemum (*Helianthemum canariense*), Mousetrap nettle (*Forsskaolea angustifolia*), and many more.

Fauna

You will come across various species of wildlife, including:
The Atlantic lizard (*Gallotia atlantica*), common rabbit (*Oryctolagus cuniculus*), the kestrel (*Falco tinnunculus*), the Southern grey shrike (*Lanius excubitor*), Berthelot's pipit (*Anthus berthelotii*), the Common linnet (*Carduelis cannabina*), Common raven (*Corvus corax*), Rock pigeon (*Columba livia*), Spanish sparrow (*Passer hispanolensis*), the Barbary partridge (*Alectoris barbara*) and the Hoopoe (*Upupa epops*), amongst many more.

Protected Natural Areas

The Protected Landscape of La Geria measures some 5,255.4 hectares and borders the municipalities of Tinajo, Tías, Yaiza, San Bartolomé and Teguise and affords incredible views of the Volcano Natural Park and Timanfaya National Park.

Alternative hiking routes

There are other trails available to walkers from the heart of La Geria which can highlight different areas of interest such as history, archaeology and the island's water and agricultural traditions.
- Fuente de Guardilama spring
- Uga via el Tablero
- El Chupadero
- Diama mountain
- Mount Gaida and Guardilama carvings
- Tegoyo and La Asomada
- Peña Paloma and Los Cuervos mountains
- Mount Negra and Mount Colorada
- Tinasoria mountain

- Taro de Testeina ancient dwellings
For further details regarding activities and

guided walks, contact:
www.senderismolanzarote.com

Advice for hikers in La Geria

Those wishing to hike in La Geria are reminded that they should always take care to stick to the network of pre-existing paths, tracks and trails. Walkers are asked to tread very carefully around the pits as the landscape is very fragile and with the slightest disturbance the rofe can slip back down the pits. On no account should people climb down the pits. It is essential that visitors respect the countryside and enjoy it fully without causing any damage.

Activities

Restaurants and bars

Bodega La Cascada restaurant, Puerto del Carmen

Hotels and rural hotels

Visitors can find a variety of excellent restaurants and bars in and around the area of La Geria. There is something for all tastes; from innovative fine dining with a touch of luxury to the more cosy traditional places for a light meal or tapas. Some of the wineries that open their doors to the public have select restaurants for those with refined tastes whilst others just offer tastings. The social-cultural clubs found all over Lanzarote also make a good choice as they generally serve typical Canarian dishes. Rural hotels also have excellent restaurants and there are other restaurants which combine traditional cuisine with more modern touches. Whichever option people choose, accompanying a meal with a Lanzarote-made wine is guaranteed to ensure a wonderful experience; gastronomy, landscape and viticulture make for a winning combination.

An excellent way to fully appreciate the natural beauty of La Geria is to opt for a stay in one of the region's rural houses or hotels. Many of these rural hotels offer luxurious accommodation in splendid old houses that have been beautifully restored to preserve traditional architecture and retain many elements which pay homage to rural life on the island. They not only have restaurants which boast organic local produce, but also health and relaxation treatments. La Geria offers peace and quiet and a unique atmosphere where visitors can stroll around in the fresh air, dine in picturesque restaurants, go on hiking trails and do sporting activities, visit wineries or simply rest whilst surrounded by beautiful scenery. It also provides an excellent base from which to explore Lanzarote's beaches and other gems.

Sports

Sunset in La Geria

With an average winter temperature that rarely dips below 18°, Lanzarote is the ideal place to do sports all year round. In fact, it's the place of choice for many elite sportsmen and women who come to Lanzarote to train. La Geria is the perfect place to go hiking, road cycling and mountain biking. For lovers of all types of mountain cycling, road races or triathlons, there are cycling routes that vary in difficulty to suit all preferences, but all of which take cyclists through beautiful scenery surrounded by vineyards and volcanoes. Apart from the Wine Run there are other sports events which pass through La Geria like the Lava Trail and the internationally renowned triathlon, Ironman. Fans of paragliding and hang gliding can also practice these sports from Mount Tinasoria near La Asomada with the added attraction of being able to enjoy a birds'-eye-view of the spectacular landscape below.

Both sunrise and sunset offer perfect moments to truly take in the beauty of La Geria's landscape. For those who are not so keen on early starts the last few hours of daylight are ideal for finding a good spot to enjoy the stunning colours of the sky as the sun goes down. The best places to enjoy the sunsets in La Geria are the La Geria winery which has a vantage point that looks out onto Timanfaya, the Rubicón winery which has great views from its terrace in the shade of a huge eucalyptus tree and the El Chupadero winery which offers an excellent selection of Lanzarote wines and tapas and is an active promoter of concerts and cultural events. It is located in the heart of La Geria and is also renowned for its famous 'Moon parties' which are organised from time to time to coincide with the full moon. www.el-chupadero.com

Events

Sonidos Líquidos
Spring

Wine Run Lanzarote
June

Photograph by Joaquín Garcia

Sonidos Líquidos is defined as a 'musical food and wine experience'. The event aims to bring together in one single event, live music, wine tasting and delicious food accompaniments. The idea is that all five senses are sated as music, wine and good food combine to create a superb atmosphere set against the stunning backdrop of the wineries in La Geria. The event started in 2010 and continues to host a calendar of concerts every which includes intimate performances in small wineries and culminates in a big concert which brings the season to an exhilarating close. The combination of great wines, music and food is a guaranteed recipe for success.

www.sonidosliquidos.com

Sports, gastronomy and nature are the key ingredients of the Lanzarote Wine Run. It is a unique race that takes participants through paths and trails in the spectacular landscape of La Geria. It takes place in the month of June and offers participants the choice between walking 10 kilometres or running 21 kilometres through vineyards and volcanic trails with refreshment stands positioned at key intervals offering wine and water. The winners get to take home their weight in litres of Lanzarote wine. The Traditional Cuisine Festival is held in La Geria over two days at the same time as the Wine Run with dozens of stalls run by producers, restaurants and wineries all offering typical Canarian and Lanzarote dishes, all of which are, of course, washed down with a selection of excellent Lanzarote wines.

www.lanzarotewinerun.com

Malvasía Lanzarote Wines Week
November

Harvest Festival
15th August

Every November sees the celebration of 'Malvasía Lanzarote Wines Week'. This annual event is when everyone associated with wine making on the island comes together and when new wines and liqueurs are presented for the first time. It is a week of workshops, seminars and presentations aimed at professionals in the wine sector. For the general public, there are courses for beginners as well as musical events. There are also wine tastings and the chance to sample cheeses, fish and vegetable dishes using local produce.

Each year the wine week is held in different municipal regions and is organised by the Regulatory Board for the Designation of Origin 'Lanzarote Wines' in conjunction with other local authority bodies, private companies and organisations.
www.dolanzarote.com

The Harvest Festival is held every year on 15th September as the grapes begin to be harvested, it also coincides with the Virgen de La Caridad festival. The event is generally celebrated in the grounds of the Bodegas La Geria and Rubicón wineries and the La Caridad chapel in the heart of the La Geria region. Visitors can see harvesting methods used in the past and appreciate how camels played an essential part of the process. The various events that take place are organised by the wineries and local town halls and include wine tastings, special menus and groups of folk music players and singers. It makes for a wonderful festive occasion with the chance to ride a camel, help pick grapes and even tread grapes.

Events

Los Dolores Fiesta
September

Saborea Lanzarote ('Tasting Lanzarote Wine and Food Festival')
December

Photograph by Adriel Perdomo

The most popular pilgrimage in Lanzarote is dedicated to the Virgin of Los Dolores and takes place in Mancha Blanca in the middle of September. According to legend, the statue of this Virgin was paraded through the streets and helped stop the lava flow from the historical eruptions in the 18th century. There are performances by folkloric groups and other activities over several days in her honour. Part of the Dolores Festival is the Nanino Díaz Cutilla Folkloric Festival and the Artisan Fair which brings together hundreds of artisans and associations that represent an array of artisan skills such as food, wine making, woodcraft, fishing, stone craft, clothing and design, jewellery making etc. The aim of the fair is to promote Canarian arts and crafts which is so rich in skill and tradition and steeped in ethnographic, historical and sustainable values.

www.artesaniadelanzarote.com

The food and wine festival *Saborea Lanzarote*, or 'Tasting Lanzarote' is held at the beginning of December in Teguise. Local agricultural producers, restaurateurs, wineries and other members of the food trade come together in a huge celebration of the island's food and drink and offer visitors the chance to sample their wares. Local wines are a huge presence and most of the wineries have stands with a selection of their wines. The festival is the big gastronomic event of the year and takes place over two days with talks, show cooking demonstrations, workshops, wine and food tasting, talks for professionals and cookery lessons for children. Throughout the year *Saborea Lanzarote* also organises themed weeks which focus on a specific aspect or component of Lanzarote cuisine such as: cheese, tuna, lentils, black pork and goat.

www.saborealanzarote.org

Culture and training

Popular Fiestas

Photograph by Miguel Cabrera

La Geria is also a social and economically vibrant setting which hosts cultural and educational activities. Nearly every week there are concerts, talks, courses, promotional events and presentations. One of the organisations that is most actively involved in the region is the Regulatory Board for the Designation of Origin 'Lanzarote Wines' which organises many activities that focus on promoting wine and providing training for professionals and those with a keen interest in wine making. The wineries that offer guided tours also hold cultural events related to wine, including concerts, book presentations and art exhibitions as well as workshops and activities that revolve around local cuisine. La Geria is also home to associations and collectives, restaurants and rural hotels and social-cultural centres which often host festivals and leisure activities for locals and visitors alike.

The period from the spring to the beginning of autumn sees an intense and peculiarly Lanzarote-style season of local festivals or *fiestas* in towns all over the island, including all the villages in and around La Geria. Some of the festivals are religious and some are held to celebrate agricultural or marine traditions. They normally involve processions and Mass, as well as cultural and social events like concerts and live performances. All of the fiestas share a picturesque backdrop and authentic atmosphere. An event especially related to wine is the Fiesta Aguapata de El Islote which takes place at the beginning of October and features the long-awaited donkey race and copious quantities of *aguapata* - the Canarian name given to low alcohol wine which is fermented very quickly after harvesting.

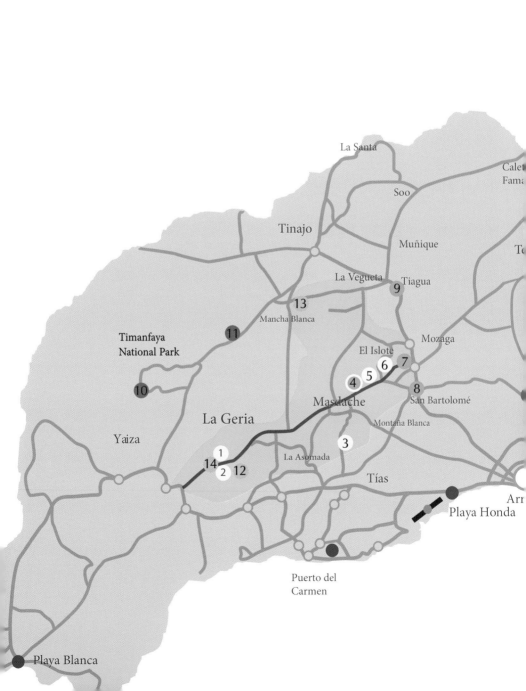

	Wine growing region
	Winery open to the public
	Winery & museum
	Museum
	Cultural & tourist centre
	Other
▬	LZ-30 main road (in La Geria)
▬	Suggested hikes and walking routes
▬	Recommended hike

1   Bodegas La Geria winery
2   Bodegas Rubicón winery
3   Bodegas Vega de Yuco winery
4   Bodegas El Grifo – Wine Museum
5   Bodegas Los Bermejos winery
6   Bodegas La Florida winery
7   Monumento al Campesino /
    Monument to Farm Wokers
8   Tanit Museum
9   El Patio Farming Museum
10 Timanfaya National Park
11 Visitors Centre
12 El Chupadero Restaurant
13 Los Dolores Church
14 Ermita La Caridad Chapel
15 César Manrique Foundation
16 Jardín de Cactus / Cactus Gardens
17 Castillo de San José Contemporary
    Art Museum
18 Cueva de los Verdes caves
19 Jameos del Agua subterranean lava
    cavern and lake
20 Mirador del Río vantage point
21 Museo de la Piratería / Pirate Museum

Acknowledgements

With gratitude to Paloma Quesada, Francisco de León, the Regulatory Board for the Designation of Origin (D.O) 'Lanzarote Wines', the Department of Agriculture and Economic Promotion of the Lanzarote Cabildo, Miguel Ángel Martín, Víctor Medina, Miguel Ángel Ferrer, Neftali Acosta, José de León, César Manrique Foundation, Bodega Cascada restaurant, Samantha Coker and Zoë Dale. With special thanks to all those who have contributed to this edition.

With the support of

The Regulatory Board for the Designation of Origin (D.O) 'Lanzarote Wines'

With the collaboration of

Central de Reservas, Lanzarote

San Bartolomé town Hall

Yaiza town Hall